VOICES IN THE RAIN

Meaning in Psychosis

A Memoir

By

Marcia A. Murphy

WIPF & STOCK · Eugene, Oregon

Wipf and Stock Publishers
199 W 8th Ave, Suite 3
Eugene, OR 97401

Voices in the Rain
Meaning in Psychosis
By Murphy, Marcia
Copyright©2010 by Murphy, Marcia
ISBN 13: 978-1-5326-5400-8
Publication date 3/21/2018
Previously published by Eagle Book Bindery Publishing Co., 2010

*But for you who revere my name, the sun of righteousness will rise
with healing in its wings.*

Malachi 4:2a

Acknowledgments

    I am grateful for the many people who helped make this book possible. Cheeni Rao, J.C. Hallman, and Sarah Townsend, Ph.D., provided expert analysis and editorial advice. Kathryn Rhett, James McKean, Ph.D., and Fritz McDonald provided instruction. Heidi Siemens-Rhodes, M.Div., and Margalea Warner provided insightful critiques. I thank David M. Kirkman for his valuable input. Glenys Williams, MD, Twila Finkelstein, and the St. Andrew Prayer Ministry gave encouragement and support. The Reverend Kyle R. Otterbein shared his perspective and knowledge. Jean McCarty, RN, provided information. I also wish to thank Marjorie Cantor, Ph.D., Richard and Penny Watson, and Virginia Spalding.
    I thank my family for the permission granted to me to use material needed to clarify difficult circumstances related to the narrative.
    Finally, I wish to express my gratitude to Russell Noyes, Jr., MD, without whose support this book would literally not have come about: thank you for your editorial suggestions and guidance to teachers in the literary arts; but, most of all, thank you for sticking by me through years of trials, for persevering and, for fighting the good fight.

Author's Note

This is a true story. However, in order to protect the privacy of individuals involved, some names, characteristics, and locations have been altered. The exceptions are names of prominent figures and those known to the public.

PROLOGUE

"WHAT ARE *YOU* DOING HERE?!" blasted a young, red-haired man in white trousers and shirt.

The dentist had had a bad day. It was 4:30; I must have been his last patient. His manner was out-of-place but being caught off guard I was too stunned to retaliate. Stumbling over my words I tried to explain why I had come to the hospital dental clinic. I thought this a common practice.

"I don't...don't have a car and I live nearby, so I was able to walk. I...I needed a place that would accept Medicaid. Most dentists won't."

For a while I had taken the bus to a dental office downtown but it was eventually rebuilt on the south side and became too difficult to reach. I knew the hospital clinic would take my insurance.

In the dental chair, my head on the rest, I turned to see the irate man. The dental assistant, a slender brunette in her mid-twenties, stood with a tense expression on her face.

"I'm Dr. Grant. You've put on the personal information form that you take the drug Risperdal. What's that for?" he asked.

"It's a psychiatric medication," I said softly.

"What's it *for*? Have you been *psychotic? Depressed?*"

He emphasized the last words by raising his voice and spewing out his questions.

"It's for schizophrenia."

There. I had said it. Now they would see me as the embodiment of deviance. I wanted to slide off the chair and crawl out the door. The dentist frowned.

"Well, what do you want?! Why are you here?!"

"I'd like to get my teeth examined and cleaned," I murmured.

"We can do that," his voice softened. "I'm leaving Iowa; you're my last patient before I pull up stakes and leave this clinic. I can't stand the winters here. I'm from Florida," he said.

I looked out the window at the buildings and trees and appreciated the sunny day. I thought how I liked Iowa. Dr. Grant and his assistant came to my side and performed an exam and cleaning. At one point he commented in a calm, almost cordial way, "You have nice teeth."

*

This is a story of submergence and emergence, of oppression and release, of search and discovery. It is a story of hope, that a life once nearly destroyed, lost, and forgotten, is brought up from the depths by an outstretched hand.

I am that life, falling, drowning, crushed. I am that life, fighting, surviving, and seeking. Rising once again, finding air, set free, soaring through the heavens—a shooting star, one among many in the brilliant night sky.

I am the girl who left her troubled home to join a cult. I am the young woman who began to hear voices yet was unable to communicate her terror. I am the psychiatric patient, lover, wife, and friend, searching for hope, recovery, and a reason to live.

Schizophrenia began in my high school years, then a psychosis erupted while I was in the Unification Church—the cult of Reverend Sun Myung Moon. I would go through numerous hospitalizations, diverse occupations, and broken relationships, before finding a new life.

My mind in its broken state was unable to think coherently, unable to process information. Gradually, through time, it began to function once again, and I rebuilt my intellect, word by word, book by book. Poverty brought added hardship, sometimes more difficult to bear than the illness that caused it. Emotional starvation and depression filled my days as I was rejected by friends and strangers—stigmatized by society.

Eventually, by seeking answers to questions many would have considered unanswerable, I began to see a way out of the labyrinth that had held me captive. All signs pointed to the psychosis which was at once the origin of my pain as well as the key to the mystery. With this train of thought I did extensive reading and wrote papers that combined spirituality and medicine, looking at mental illness from a holistic perspective. I also wrote about how it feels to be treated as less than human by society and about the discovery of places where I found joyful fellowship and a sense of well-being. As a result of my search and the changes it brought, my life became rich in manifold and unexpected ways.

To reach the point in my life where I was able to write and function in a normal fashion, I first had to go through years of turmoil that began as a teen. It was then, feeling lost and alone, I joined the cult. That costly error led me, by a series of events, to a sojourn through hell, a sojourn I survived only by the grace of God.

CHAPTER 1

"Would you like to come to a lecture on world peace tonight at Schaeffer Hall? It's at seven. Can you come?"

The sky was overcast and with a biting February wind at my face, I passed along an icy sidewalk near the University campus. The street was lined with a hodgepodge of store buildings dating from the late 1800's to the present painted modern hues of pink, brown, gray, and white with complements of red brick here and there.

A young man in his early thirties, speaking with a German accent, invited me to an introductory meeting of his religious organization. He said the presentation would cover religion, politics, and world unity. We spoke briefly and he handed me a brochure; then I walked away.

That evening, I ventured into the frigid air again. Short winter days brought nightfall as a shroud over the campus. I found Schaeffer Hall and with great effort pulled open the heavy entrance door, went up the stairway and to the first door on the left.

Among the rows of desks students from all walks of life sat or stood conversing. A man with short trim hair and polo shirt braced himself against the wall as he gave the petite blond a mischievous smile. A stringy haired Dylan fan, displaying Bob's latest tour on his t-shirt, snuffed out his cigarette on a mounted pencil sharpener then tossed the butt onto the linoleum. A hefty woman with a mass of curled hair plopped a stack of books on the desktop before squeezing into her seat, adjusting her wire-rim glasses and letting out a loud sigh.

I hesitated, took a step back, and was about to retreat the way I had come when I was greeted by the man from the street and was soon surrounded by a group of people. They spoke with foreign accents and I asked where they were from. The man from the street, named Dietrich, said Germany. Two responded from France, one England, and two were from Holland. They smiled and welcomed me enthusiastically, asking if I were a student or employed. I told them I was a freshman in college. Other invited guests floated in, intermingled, then we all gravitated toward desks.

Behind the podium Dietrich began to discuss philosophical principles interspersed with spirituality including some Christian doctrine. He was of medium height and wore calf-high black leather boots with his beige trousers tucked in and an ivory sweater. His thinning brown hair was swept back over his head and he had a prominent nose and sharply defined mouth. I found his accent attractive and as he spoke he directed the pointer toward bold-faced words on a poster board.

"Mankind is in a state of spiritual ignorance. What has caused this condition?" Dietrich asked. "It's true, religions have tried to alleviate the darkness that covers the earth. But, even though practiced by many, these religions have not gotten rid of wickedness; there is still evil in all parts of the world."

Dietrich coughed, briefly putting his hand to his mouth and the Dylan fan lit up again. The lecture captured my imagination.

"Where did human beings come from? Where are they going? What is the purpose of life? Is there a God? What happens when we die? How can good and evil be defined? If you are seeking answers to these questions and solutions to the problems of spiritual ignorance, where will you find them, those that satisfy your inner most being?"

I listened attentively and after the hour-long presentation Dietrich approached me as I headed toward the door. Stepping near, he placed his hand on my arm and I felt flustered, at a loss for words.

"Would you like to come to our city headquarters to hear the rest of the lecture series?"

It was nearly 8pm. Sue, an American member with an oval face and ponytail, stood beside him pleading with me to go with the group.

"You'll really find the rest of the presentations interesting! Why don't you ride in our van? We can take you home later," she said.

I was flattered and took their kindness at face value. It did not occur to me that they were anything other than friendly people who had my best interests at heart. I went with them to an apartment ten minutes from campus.

The center was located on the second floor of a modern apartment building. Once inside Sue asked me to sit on the floor beside her and the others. The bare walls and draped windows had an off-yellow tinge. In a corner sat a plain looking table and set of chairs but, other than that, there was no other furniture. Spotted, streaked, and torn, the carpet must have once been "treated" by a cat, undoubtedly belonging to a former tenant. With the décor unpretentious, I relaxed. No need to put on airs; I could be myself.

Bending and stretching to set up poster boards covered with diagrams, Dietrich gave a continuation of his presentation on campus. He called his teaching "The Divine Principle," a creation of the organization's founder. At this point I did not know who the founder was; much was still a mystery. I struggled to listen as Dietrich droned on, barely keeping my eyes open. Then, at midnight, he stopped speaking. I thought the material he presented interesting but the ideas had little impact. I was more impressed by the way the people treated me—like I was important and special. Their tone of voice was kind and gentle and they looked into my eyes and waited patiently for me to respond to their questions. This was unlike what I had been used to at home.

*

"*Fermez la bouche!*"

This was Bonnie's response when I protested her borrowing of my blue dress for school that morning. Since I had sewed it myself the dress was special so I was particularly offended. My family had just finished dinner and I stopped my sister on her way to practice the clarinet.

"What does that mean? *Fermezzz la*...? I don't know French; speak to me in plain English."

"Shut your mouth. Now—*allez-vous en!*"

She abruptly turned her back, her long blond ponytail swishing to the side. After walking to her room she slammed the door. With Bonnie, it was sibling rivalry. Deep down we still loved each other even if we seemed out of touch with that emotion.

Bonnie, ever-popular, was voted Paper Doll Queen by the junior high and, in high school, was a candidate for Homecoming royalty. I tried to emulate her outgoing nature at school.

For a moment as I faced Bonnie's closed door, I recalled having seen my best friend, Stephanie, at school that day. She was a member of the swim team and an honor student. As she stood by her locker with her boyfriend laughter seemed to bubble out of her without effort and, clearly, with joy. By contrast I felt a deadness inside, a flat emptiness that lacked variation from one day to the next. I wondered how Stephanie could so easily express her delight and, as I passed, I lifted my hand and waved, barely managing a smile. I couldn't laugh. I couldn't remember the last time I had. I thought I had lost the ability.

Conceding victory to Bonnie with her superior battle plan, I walked to the livingroom and over to the Magnavox Hi-Fi. My older brother, Stewart, had left his Beatles' album, *Rubber Soul*, lying nearby. It was one of my favorites so I played it, sitting cross-legged on the carpet, my face toward the speaker. From somewhere in the back of the house my parents yelled at each other. I could not tell what they were fighting about; I just heard an occasional obscenity. As a result the soothing effect of the music was only partial; then suddenly, it was destroyed altogether.

"Turn that music off!"

At the crack of a switch the canned laughter of *Hogan's Heroes* erupted from the television set. I jumped up and rushed over to my younger brother.

"Scott! Turn that down! Why do you always have to— ?"

"Turn off the music!" He started shouting, calling me insulting names, then leaned back on the gold corduroy couch and stretched out his legs. Flakes of mud fell from his Converse All-Stars onto a striped and paisley pillow. I sought the support of my parents but heard scuffling in the kitchen.

"I'll leave, Tim! I'll go—

"To Chicago? Again? Sure, sure you will," my father said.

"I don't have to put up with this!" my mother cried out.

She wanted to drive away again, away from a marriage and family that offered little comfort. And I couldn't blame her. She felt trapped and overburdened. At work, as a clinical psychologist, she took care of emotionally ill patients then came home to a man she could no longer get along with and children who bickered unceasingly.

I heard my father's heavy footsteps going back to the bedroom where he went in and softly closed the door. I entered the kitchen where stacks of dirty dishes lined the beige Formica counter. The sweet scent of dinner's bar-b-qued ribs filled the air and tupperware containers half-filled with mashed potatoes and corn sat ready for their tops.

Mom, tall and slender, stood next to the stove wiping her face with Kleenex and pushed her stylish red hair back from her forehead. After glancing at me she reached for her leather purse and car keys near the phone but hesitated.

"Blast," she said after looking down at open-toed slippers on her stocking feet. When, finally, she sat down I went and stood in front of her.

"Mom, I wanted to listen to music. Scott comes in and turns on the TV! Every night, it's like this every night—I can't get any peace and quiet. And the TV's always too loud, make him turn it down! I learned in psychology class that constant, bombastic noise—

Something made me stop. My mother's breathing became fast, her face once pink, became red. As her forehead furrowed she squeezed her eyes shut and from their corners tears started to fall again. Suddenly, she leapt to her feet and struck the air with her fist, a finger pointing toward the kitchen sink.

"Wash the dishes!" she screamed.

My mother took a step toward me and started in on my lax work habits and disrespectful attitude. I talked back all the while.

"Why is it that the only time you ever speak to me is when you're yelling? Can't we ever have a normal, calm conversation?"

My mother took another step closer and glared, now with both hands spread in the air.

"You can go to hell!"

*

"It's too late for you to go home now. Why don't you stay here with us tonight? We have more to talk over," Sue said.

I only hesitated a second before answering.

"Okay, I guess I could. I'm kind of tired."

I felt no fear. They were such nice people.

Before getting into sleeping bags on the floor, with men and women segregated in different rooms, Sue and the others continued to talk with me about their teachings and asked me about myself. I enjoyed their attention but now it started to seem odd that from the time I had arrived I had not been out of their sight or left alone to think. Someone even walked with me to the bathroom and back again.

The next morning we were awakened by the sound of music. I had only gotten about three hours of sleep and the hard floor had been uncomfortable. Breakfast consisted of raw oatmeal mixed with chocolate chips, coconut flakes, and milk. Before eating Dietrich had the group stand in a circle to sing and pray.

I had no idea where all this was headed; my mind was not clear. I followed directions. Dietrich and Sue convinced me to stay longer to hear more about their organization. By mid-day I was hungry and desperately needed rest. But after lunch I was again swept along with more group activities that left me little opportunity to reflect.

The warmth of my new friends and the attention they showered on me was a welcome change from the dreary isolation I had experienced at home. Soon I did not want to return home where I had felt ill at ease. There were no other relatives I felt comfortable with and I could not think of anyone to visit. But here were smiling, happy people interested in me. They liked me. So that afternoon when they pressed me to join their group the decision was easy.

"Would you stay and become a member?" Dietrich asked and his eyes studied my face.

"Yes."

Sue gave me a hug.

"That's great!" she said.

"Do you have any savings you'd like to donate? All new members give their cash," Dietrich said with a serious tone.

"I don't have much but I'll give you what I have."

I took $15 from my purse and handed it to him.

"Thanks, Marcia. I'll drive you to your house and we'll take a suitcase of your clothes. We're leaving soon for central Iowa."

*

Dietrich, I soon discovered, had plans for me. I was his "spiritual child;" he was my "spiritual father." I left with him and eight others for central Iowa where we spent the next two weeks in another college town. By getting me out of Iowa City as soon as possible he removed me from the environment I had grown up in. I would later learn that this was the group's way of separating me from my present, my past, my identity. It was the beginning of an indoctrination which was to weaken my self-confidence and destroy my individuality.

But why would I willingly give up my freedom to join? What made me susceptible to their recruitment tactics? J.M. Curtis and M.J. Curtis state in *Factors Related to Susceptibility and Recruitment by Cults,* that young people who feel rejected and abandoned by their families often feel worthless, frightened, confused, powerless, and alone. Cults act as surrogate families, offering social support and fulfilling unmet needs. When the chance came to leave a family I thought had rejected me, I chose to disappear.

*

Dietrich recruited a professor's daughter who could have passed for a fashion model. She became the focus of his attention. I felt slighted and grew jealous. She was an artist and her quirky, unorthodox manner stole his heart. Relationships like this within the group were strictly platonic. I became emotionally attached to charismatic personalities such as Dietrich. This was the main reason I stayed involved.

Daily life began with morning devotions in an empty bedroom that had a small cloth-covered table at one end. In the center stood the photo of a middle-aged Asian man and his wife. Members kneeled or sat on their heels in rows. At any given time one or another of us bowed to the floor. Usually, Dietrich said the first prayer kneeling at the front and facing the photo.

"True Parents, we bow down to you and beseech you to defeat the powers of Satan and we ask that you save the United States from the evil forces bent on its destruction."

I learned that the "True Parents" were the people in the photo.

"Because we are weak," Dietrich continued, "we need your strength. Use us as instruments to find your lost children and to build the kingdom of heaven on earth. Guide us to those you have chosen to be a part of your church. Increase our numbers!"

After a while Dietrich would stop and instruct the rest of us to pray out loud. Our words were similar to his but many men and women cried out passionately, shedding tears, and gesticulating with their hands. At the end of our prayers we did not close with "Amen," instead, we were taught to say, "In the name of the True Parents."

The True Parents turned out to be the Korean founder of the Unification Church, Reverend Sun Myung Moon and his wife.

*

Sun Myung Moon was born in 1920 in Pyungan Bukedo province of northwestern Korea and his family converted to Christianity when he was ten years old. At the age of sixteen he claimed to have had a vision and was instructed to restore the earth, thereby bringing about the physical kingdom of God. Before acting on this vision and starting his public ministry in 1946, he studied electrical engineering in Seoul and later at Tokyo's Waseda University. After returning to Korea He developed the movement's text, *The Divine Principle*, and a missionary follower to the United States was the first to translate Moon's writings into English in 1963. They contained philosophical and theological ideas including many references to the Bible.

Moon made his first visit to the United States in 1965. Later, in 1971, he purchased a home in New York and that was followed by a rapid spread of his organization with a dramatic increase in membership. During the sixties, the Unification Church had movements on both coasts spawned by the early missionaries from Korea. The east had an orthodox theological interpretation of Moon's *Principle*, whereas the west, called the "Oakland Family," was less theological and more humanistic. The United States created its own leaders who were trained by the foreign missionaries.

When Moon started the Unification Church in Korea he proclaimed himself Lord of the Second Advent, a concept borrowed from the Christian religion. But deviating from Christianity he taught that he, as the Messiah, and his wife (claiming they were both perfect) would create perfect children and adopt spiritual children—cult members—to establish the kingdom of heaven on earth. At what point in my indoctrination I began to believe this, I do not know. When I joined, these beliefs were not my concern. Since I was told to end prayers "In the name of the True Parents," I did so.

We began daily activities on campus by extending invitations to students to attend presentations. Approaching individuals sitting alone, eating or studying, we handed them fliers and struck up conversations. A few attended the evening lecture and then some joined the church.

All activity was directed by the leader, in our case, Dietrich. Before we retired at midnight the common practice was to gather for more prayer. Members, exhausted from working all day, had little time for personal reflection. Except for witnessing (recruiting), members were cut off from the world and not allowed to read newspapers, magazines, or books, except those published by the church. Radios and televisions were prohibited. Within the church education was scorned and any kind of self-development discouraged. But there wasn't time for such things anyway. Dietrich saw to it that we were always kept busy.

One evening after members had eaten dinner, Dietrich told us to gather on the floor around him. He had boosted himself onto a table; his legs were dangling over the side and swinging back and forth. I seated myself at the side of the group in eager anticipation and, when Dietrich's steely gaze fell upon me I felt flattered. I had not made other friends in the church because when I wasn't working I was reading books. I had forgotten how to relate to people. Even though Dietrich rarely spoke to me now, I saw him as my only friend so I especially sought to please him.

A shrill whistle sliced through the air drawing silence. Then Dietrich began to address the group.

"Father has directed us to leave Iowa and go to Minnesota."

Father was Reverend Moon.

"The Divine Principle says that leaders are subjects and other members of the church are objects. Objects must always obey subjects. Since I am your subject you must be obedient objects and do what I say."

"Simply stop thinking," he continued. "You must swear total allegiance to Father. He is the central figure whom I obey and I am the central figure whom you must obey. In whatever situation you find yourself, whether it be my group or someone else's, always follow the central figure and do not question his authority."

Commands such as these had a strong impact. Later I would find that to the outside world Unification Church members appeared as mindless zombies under a spell. Moon, by demanding complete submission, made all career and life decisions for his followers so that they became like puppets. Thus, in varying degrees, his followers gave up their own will and self-determination.

Curtis and Curtis further state that in addition to lack of family support, a weak ego or sense of identity may contribute to involvement in cults. Without a strong sense of self, powerful persons, they suggest, may dominate and persuade an individual to do their bidding. At that point in my life I was not an independent, strong-willed individual, confident of my abilities and with a strong sense of purpose.

Dietrich spoke for another ten minutes before ordering us to do our studies. Always, after dinner, we read Moon's writings. Some of these described the church's ideological goal of bringing the world's scientists and theologians together to seek unification according to Moon's Divine Principle.

On we went from Iowa to Minnesota. In Minneapolis, I was initiated into the practice of fundraising. In suburban neighborhoods we took boxes of candles house to house and were told to say, "We are raising money for a Christian youth counseling center." This was not true but Dietrich held that the end justifies the means; he said we should use "heavenly deception" to sell our products. So in order to raise money, we promised to help troubled youth. I was without a conscience and followed his directions. We worked from morning until after dark but were not allowed to keep any money for ourselves. I did this work joylessly in sub-zero weather only to gain Dietrich's approval.

In the spring we returned to Iowa, this time to a small northern town where we continued witnessing and fundraising. One day, Dietrich asked me to sit with him in the center's kitchen. After pouring ourselves coffee we pulled up chairs and sat facing each other across the table. I was tense with excitement; Dietrich had singled me out.

"Marcia, members have to spend three years in the church before they can get married; Father chooses the partners. Do you think you'd like to get married some day?"

"Yes, definitely," I said. I was, of course, hoping I could marry *him*.

"Another requirement for marriage is a seven-day fast. This shows Father that you have the dedication and self-discipline to qualify for the privileged position of husband or wife," Dietrich said. "Do you understand what I'm saying?"

"Yes."

"During the fast you are not allowed anything to eat or drink except water; you are expected to complete the day's work with the rest of the group; and you must pray an extra hour mornings and evenings on top of the usual routine.

"Fasting promotes spiritual growth," he said. "By doing this an individual pays indemnity and cancels past sins, drawing near to God."

"What do you mean by 'pays indemnity'?" I asked.

"All people sin against God and in this way damage their relationship with Him," Dietrich said. "So in order for that relationship to be restored every human has to pay a price for their sin which is called indemnity. When this is paid people are redeemed and once again have a right relationship with God."

I sipped my coffee. This teaching opposed what I had learned in the Christian church that Jesus Christ paid for mankind's sins on the cross. He paid the full price and faith in Him saves us, not some action of our own.

"I'll do it," I said.

I decided to start the next morning. Going without breakfast seemed simple but towards lunchtime my hunger pains could only be silenced by an abundance of water. Since we witnessed in the student union part of the time I was able to obtain glasses of ice water from the cafeteria. As I sat at a table sipping my bland refreshment the aroma of hamburger, pizza, and other good things filled the air so I left to avoid temptation. I headed to the library where I felt certain I would find the intellectually curious, people who might be interested in hearing a lecture.

The next several days I focused on church work with a strange absence of hunger. I decided to just put thoughts of food out of my mind since eating was off limits. But on the last morning I was in a physically fragile state and was unable to rise with the others. At some point, sensing their absence, I gathered my strength to stand, then dressed and brushed my teeth. I heard prayers in the next room and went to join them. Kneeling at the back of the room I grew lightheaded and faint.

"You're late!" Dietrich scolded, his voice reminding me of Nazi soldiers in WWII movies.

"Sorry," I muttered.

I bowed down and stretched my hands before me onto the floor, resting my forehead. Jumbled words about providence, kingdom, the enemy, Messiah, etc., seemed to emerge from a cloudy dim memory and I gave up on their direction. When I finished praying I told Dietrich I was too weak to participate in the usual routine but he answered that I had to at least accompany the group to campus even if I only sat in the cafeteria and drank water.

I went with the group on shaky legs but as I looked around I suddenly noticed with elation that my vision had become vivid and hearing more acute. The sunlight was now an intense white light, grass had a greenish glow, the colors of flowers were brilliant and the sky, a richer blue. Boughs of trees surrendered to the wind with the rustle of dancing leaves, the sound of a waterfall, a rushing stream. All seemed to have taken on a spiritual dimension and I somehow became hypersensitive to a distorted, yet magnified, reality. I had entered an altered state of consciousness although I did not realize it at the time.

Several factors contributed to this state of mind, one being my condition before the fast. Much of the time members did not receive sufficient nutrition. We were usually fed meager amounts—mostly cereal, rice, legumes, rarely meat—but ample amounts of sugar and coffee. Vegetables and fruits were scarce. Thus, the nutritional value of meals was poor as reflected in my future hospital records in which malnutrition was noted. Lack of proper diet can alter the mind.

It is general knowledge that fasting may bring about alterations of consciousness. Add to this the group's spiritual practices of morning and evening prayers and, eventually, my own obsessive meditative practice, and you have conditions conducive to what religious traditions describe as a mystical state. Arthur Wallis, in *GOD'S CHOSEN FAST,* states that fasting makes one "sensitive" to the spiritual world and this in turn can make one "subject to impressions and voices," which may come from a divine source or satanic one.

Though I had been told fasting would purify my soul, it actually seemed to weaken me. Fasting made me more susceptible to outside influences; I was losing will power and becoming obsessed with church doctrine as well as following orders. Moon's teachings became further embedded in my mind. In this way the church gained power over me and, instead of furthering my spiritual growth, as I had hoped it might, the fast, coupled with prayer, began to pull me into occult realms. And I was ill-prepared for what I would later find there.

CHAPTER 2

"Would you like to go to a big city…a really big city?"
Dietrich made this offer sound attractive.
"You can fly to New York, Father spends a lot of time in the area; his home is located a few miles north of Manhattan."
I thought that would be exciting, that I'd love to see New York, a focal point of the Unification Church activities. And I'd never flown on an airplane.
"Sure," I said.
The next afternoon I flew into LaGuardia and from there took a cab into Manhattan. Dietrich had given me an address on the Upper East Side which turned out to be a brownstone townhouse with broad steps leading to the front door. I let myself in and was greeted by an Asian woman in a navy skirt, white blouse, and short black hair. She smiled but didn't give her name.
"I'm from Iowa. I was told that I would be taken from here to the Belvedere estate," I said.
"I'll let Mr. Nishika know you're here," she said.
She left me standing on the marble floor of the foyer. I had never seen such a fancy place. Dark green velveteen drapes pulled back by golden braided cords fell over tall windows; carpet of the same green color covered a winding staircase. But I did not stay long. I had fixed a cup of tea and seated myself in the dining area when Mr. Nishika approached. Thin and bony,

with a narrow face, he seemed taller than the average Japanese man.

"I have arranged for you to be taken to Belvedere as planned." He sat down next to me, his voice warm. "You're very beautiful. I think Iowa must be a very beautiful place."

I didn't know what to say; I didn't feel particularly beautiful and even if I were attractive it hadn't gotten me very far in life. As he continued the conversation I thought his mastery of the English language impressive. After we talked a few minutes I left with a man who would drive me to the training center.

Approaching the estate, the car slowed to a crawl as it turned onto a cement entrance way spotted with puddles from an afternoon storm. A black iron fence surrounded the grounds and two guards stood beside a gate. My driver rolled down his window and said something to one of them, a young muscular man with a strong jaw line and crew cut. Both gave a laugh and the gate creaked open allowing us to go through. As we drove up a slight incline, a blur of yellow, brown, and black slithered across the path of the car onto the other side. It disappeared as quickly as it had come.

Great oak trees on either side of the road cast dark shadows but through their limbs I made out a mansion twice the size of the grandest upscale home in Iowa. As we got closer two shiny black cars came into view parked near the front door: a limousine and a Mercedes Benz. We passed by the mansion to the hill's crest and from there I saw three smaller buildings scattered on grounds below the size of a football field. At the bottom, the driveway curved around the perimeter. Flaking white paint on the exteriors of the buildings revealed years of neglect and a broken wooden trellis leaned to one side. Stone-crafted walkways led from each front door to the road and here and there were small shrubs and rocks. I learned that one building had been the servant's quarters, one the grounds keeper's, and the other a guest house. These had been converted into housing for the staff and other members. Top leaders lived in the mansion and had servants. Moon, his wife, and children occupied a luxurious estate in nearby Irvington.

Another building, larger than the small houses, was tucked into the side of another hill and was used as a lecture hall. Its windows were streaked with dirt and a few were broken, their sharp edges protruding like daggers in odd directions.

A great boulder, stark and solitary, lay near the top of the first hill thirty feet from the back of the mansion. It seemed to occupy a place of prominence. Members called it Holy Rock. From this place grass stretched in all directions with thick woodland bordering on three sides. The only way out was through the front gate.

As a member of the church I was considered part of the "Family" and Belvedere proved to be the church's main training center. About 70 people were there for a two week session. Many were like me, i.e., white, middle-class, in their late teens or early twenties, and had attended college. Most were from various parts of the United States, but others were from Asia. I shared sleeping quarters with about 15 women. Leaving my bags there, I joined a small a group at another building where I discovered how I was to be initiated.

At this place I met Mr. Yamikama who was Japanese, Moon's right-hand man. He had fine wispy hair and silver wire-rim glasses. He was of medium height and slight build.

Whenever Mr. Yamikama attempted to speak English his eyes would open wide and his voice took on a childish tone, one of obvious embarrassment. Switching back to Japanese his voice would deepen and sophistication would return, intelligent, smooth and rapid. I immediately fell in love with him but learned he was already married. Still, his wife remained in Japan. I was told he had been an industrialist and had amassed a fortune. I did not know why I was attracted to him, nor did I consider why, I just knew that for the time being he would take Dietrich's place in my heart. But since he was in such a high position in the church and was several years older, I felt out-classed and out-ranked.

On a few occasions, when in New York, I sought Mr. Yamikama's company and eventually a friendship of sorts developed. But he spoke through an interpreter and this prevented me from getting to know him well. As were all my relationships with men in the church this one too was platonic. However, I soon found that I was not alone in my sense of attraction. Dozens of others had fallen for him as well.

At his house that first day, Mr. Yamikama spoke about how the church wanted to present a certain image. To my dismay, he first had our hair cut short, both men and women. Even a woman with long thick hair extending to her waist lost most of it. The resulting styles were plain and simple. Second, he gave us clothes consisting of ordinary slacks with tops devoid of artistic design. Our shoes were brown leather, practical, and utilitarian.

I was hoping to catch up on sleep but every day we rose at 6am and retired at 1am. As earlier, we slept in sleeping bags on a hard floor with no pillow. Rooms were overcrowded and stuffy. Three times a day we had meals in a dining area. As before, lunch and dinner were mostly starch such as white rice with little protein. Lack of proper nutrition and rest contributed to my physical weariness and mental cloudiness. As the days passed we were bombarded with rituals and incessant group activities which further unsettled my state of mind. Everything members saw and heard in the milieu appeared to have been preplanned and organized. At no time was socializing encouraged but occasionally I had friendly conversations with others between activities.

The training center had an emotionally charged atmosphere. Leaders would call us to gather at Holy Rock and with shouts of adulation they passionately petitioned God in prayer. Then, as they finished, members were encouraged to join in with their own exuberant singing and chants. Emotions were stirred with each repetition and a sense of camaraderie was created. All such activities rushed forward making it difficult for me to think.

Moon himself gave marathon lectures lasting three or four hours. He used repetition to emphasize key points about Satan, good and evil, the Messiah and one world family. He cited biblical and historical facts though I did not know if they were accurate. With each impassioned speech my worldview underwent change.

Afternoons, members first removed their shoes and seated themselves on the floor. Father stood before us speaking Korean and, usually, Colonel Pak was at his side interpreting. Father had a very rounded and tan face with a long nose and a receding hair line. He stood about five feet, nine inches and usually wore a casual shirt with a dark suit coat and a large gold ring on his left hand. Raising and lowering the pitch of his voice for emphasis he made swift gestures with his hands. I had never heard the Korean language before and now found it captivating. There was something magnetic about Father's voice that seemed to draw me to him.

"You have a great responsibility for all of mankind! If you do not work hard for me and do exactly as I say the United States and world will be lost to Satan!

"Before you take any action, ask yourself, 'Is this action done for God and to bring about the kingdom of heaven on earth? Do I move every muscle and think every thought for God?' No second of the day can be wasted! Don't allow Satan to claim even one moment; don't allow him to invade your life!"

After wiping his brow with a handkerchief he continued shouting.

"If your physical parents try to stop you from following me you must kill them! Who will kill their parents for me?! Raise your hands!"

Most of those in the room thrust their hands into the air.

"Good, well done! No one should stand in your way....You belong to the True Parents now; you have chosen which side you are on. Each of us is either on the side of good or on the side of evil. Any individual, any family, tribe or nation—as well as the world itself—is on the side of evil or on the side of good. There are many countries in the world and each nation thinks that it is on the side of goodness. This is because any nation is a group of individuals. Individuals have the tendency to think of themselves as good so nations also have the tendency to think in like fashion. But what is the basis for defining good and evil absolutely? We know that all nations or individuals cannot be on the side of good. There must be a way to discriminate....If you know there is a boundary between good and evil then do you find yourself having gone across to join the side of good? You, yourself, know the answer very well....Are you on the side of the True Parents?"

After lectures members gathered in small groups on the hill outside and, there, a leader held discussions. Later, we had more group prayers and singing, repeating the morning rituals. As the training progressed Moon gained psychological control over my mind and in complying with his instructions I turned myself over to him. Thoughts and actions were no longer my own, but his. And, in this way, my life became a sacrifice for the movement.

There was pressure to conform. I found that if I expressed negative opinions I was treated as an outcast. So in order to obtain affection and approval I sought to please the leaders. Even though little praise was given it was all I lived for. I was happy to receive any crumbs that might fall from the table.

As the days passed I lost confidence in my decision making ability for my aim was to do only as I was told. Gradually, I became as dependent as a child, no longer functioning as an adult.

Near the end of training after a day of tiring lectures, I went to Holy Rock to pray. All was quiet as I walked up the hill alone. It was a clear summer night; stars were out and a quarter moon shone. I knelt on the hardened earth rimming the boulder, a gray rock nearly seven feet across and curving up to around four feet in height. As I had during my teen years using Transcendental Meditation, I now sought a spiritual reality that I hoped would lead me to God. I clasped my hands resting them on the cool rock and sang the Lord's Prayer, a song I had heard my father sing when I was young. Through its melodious words I felt my spirit go beyond the earthly compound to commune with God.

"And deliver us from evil...."

At the song's conclusion I walked down the hill and was enveloped once again by the blackness of night.

The next morning Moon had members gather in rows behind the mansion. He then divided us into groups, each with an Asian man and woman as the team leader and "mother." The leader was to drive a van and direct fundraising; the mother prepared meals and did laundry.

Moon strode up and down the rows tapping selected people on the shoulder and yelling to the crowd, his translator not far behind.

"You will go fundraising across the United States for me! Each of you must make at least a hundred dollars a day! You are doing God's work! When customers buy your products they are paying indemnity for their sins and will be saved!"

*

From Tarrytown my group headed south through Washington, D.C., then down to New Orleans and Dallas. Continuing westward, we stopped in cities and towns along the way. In my mind I knew only to work, to follow orders. As the distance grew between me and Mr. Yamikama and Dietrich I forced myself to forget about them and, instead, I became mechanical, focusing on only fundraising goals. I also forgot about my appearance, something I had been obsessed with before joining the Unification Church. Now it did not matter how I looked; I just put on clothes the church bought me. I cared little for my hair, its short style easy to brush and ignore. With a slightly athletic build and average figure I neither stood out nor attracted attention.

We usually slept nights in church centers or occasionally in a budget motel with all the women in one room and the leader in another. As in the past we rose at 6am but now did not retire until two in the morning. On different days we sold roses or carnations, scented candles in brandy snifters or boxes of chocolate-covered mints. We went door to door in suburbs and at shopping malls we solicited in parking lots. But when it was too late to be in the suburbs and the malls closed we sold products to patrons of bars.

One night I took an elevator in a high-rise office building to a top floor nightclub. As I entered I was engulfed in smoke which soon filled my lungs. The Eagles sang from a jukebox lit up with colored lights and raucous laughter stabbed through the hum of conversations. I saw a portly man with greasy hair, wearing a business suit, sitting at the bar. As I approached him he put a cigarette to his mouth and poured wine into his glass. After whispering to the bleached-blond sitting next to him they burst into laughter and she slapped him on the back.

Gripping my bucket of roses very tightly I looked into the man's face. He grinned, revealing uneven teeth, one with a gold cap.

"Hi, would you like to buy a flower? It's for a good cause, a religious organization. We help—

"Hey, look at this, Jane! Isn't she cute?"

He nudged the blond with his elbow.

She looked at me, threw back her head and howled, punching the man's arm.

"Buy me some flowers, Sam," she said. "Come on, do it."

"How much do you want for a flower, kid? No—how much for the whole bucket?!"

The man and woman turned, looked at each other, and after a second's pause exploded once again into laughter. I glanced around the room and discovered I had become the center of attention.

"All the roses? A hundred dollars for the whole bunch!"

It was a long shot but I thought I'd try my luck. After all, what did I have to lose?

At once the man dug into his wallet and pulled out a wad from which he selected two 50's that he held in front of me.

"There you go, babe!" he said and laughed.

I put the bucket on the counter and grabbed the money.

"Thanks, have a good evening!" I said and quickly left.

Later I tried to impress the team with my story but as it turned out most had earned two or three hundred dollars that same day.

When work ended we took great care in counting the money, straightening out wrinkled bills then stacking them neatly. Once, while counting, I passed out and fell to the floor. I had been hungry and exhausted but upon rising the next morning the same hectic pace continued. Financial quotas had to be met and according to our leader little else mattered.

None of the other women became my friends. For some unknown reason we failed to connect. Often, team leaders transferred friends to different units in distant states which suggested that emotional attachments were discouraged. Except for an occasional phone call I was no longer in contact with Dietrich. To compensate for the lack of relationships I concentrated on reading church literature as the van traveled from state to state. But the emotional distance between me and church members proved crippling; I was lonely, starving for affection and thought I had no where else to go.

CHAPTER 3

The tablets were bitter and hard to swallow but I managed to get them down. At sixteen years of age I had had enough of life.

"Bonnie…Bonnie…open the door. I have to talk to you."

"What do you want? It's late."

Bonnie leaned against the door frame in a lavender nightgown with jumbo curlers in her hair, the book *Native Son* in one hand.

"I ate a bottle of aspirin; I need help."

My vision started to blur and I felt a burning sensation in my stomach.

"Marcia! You're kidding! What'd you do that for? Do you mean baby aspirin?"

"No, the adult Bayer. There's at least a hundred in a bot—"

"I have to tell Mom!"

After throwing her book on the desk she ran down the hall and burst into my parents' room. I heard a flurry of voices and commotion.

Soon I was hunched over in the back seat of the car with Mom driving and my sister next to her. I leaned my face on the scratchy upholstery, kept my eyes shut and listened to the ringing in my ears. I shivered in my navy pea coat which hung open.

At the hospital both of them jumped out and sped toward the emergency entrance. I remained slouched on the back seat and my mind started to drift into a thick, gray fog. Feeling abandoned once again, the emotional turmoil I had experienced at home became magnified and the desire to end my life returned.

"She's still in the car!" I heard in a distance.

The car door opened and someone dragged me out. With feeble steps and people holding both arms, I entered a brightly lit bare room with white walls. After I climbed on top of a table a strange man in a white coat forced a tube down my nose. Then my eyes rolled back and I blacked out.

After what must have been a short time I awoke in a hospital room and started to cry. The pain in my stomach was extreme and the ringing in my ears had intensified. I reached up and felt dried blood caked around my nose. Illumination from a small light helped me make out my mother approaching, her coat over one arm. When she stopped at my bed she was breathing heavily and gasped before she spoke.

"Why did you do this, Marcia? It's so expensive!"

I didn't answer, her words crushed me. I glanced at her tired face and continued crying. Her response to the overdose was to take me to see a therapist, a psychiatric nurse. But I didn't think that I needed therapy. What I needed was for my family to care about me, to make home life bearable and give me strength to meet life's challenges. But I soon found that the psychiatric nurse was to become important to me, more than my emotionally distant family.

Tempers continued to flare unpredictably and moods shifted without apparent reason resulting in verbal abuse. This perpetuated the instability that was a part of our everyday lives.

*

The leader usually stopped at the city hall to obtain a solicitor's permit. But he also told us to ignore "No Soliciting" signs and we often peddled without a license. One night while I was selling carnations in downtown Los Angeles a police car pulled up beside me. Two uniformed officers got out and one said, "Young lady, may I see your selling permit?"

"I don't have one."

Suddenly afraid, I hoped they would just give me a warning, tell me to stop selling and let it go at that.

"You're coming with us! We're taking you in."

He took my elbow, escorted me to the car and nudged me through the door. I felt in a state of shock during the ride to the police station. I had been arrested but did not feel like a criminal.

They put me in a jail cell with women who appeared to be "ladies of the night," and I expected to be there a while. I remembered Father saying, "Don't allow Satan to claim even one second of your life. Keep working for God."

Recalling the book of Matthew in the Bible where Jesus taught that the greatest among you will be a servant of all, I decided to scrub the floor. I took a rag that I found near the sink, wetted it, and got down on my hands and knees cleaning the cement floor much to the amusement of my cell mates. I scrubbed with blind force, compelled, unthinking, like someone driven to perform. Oblivious to the barbs from the ladies I exhausted myself in the effort then sat in a corner too ill at ease to close my eyes. I suspect my cellmates concluded that I was a fanatic. In a few hours my leader bailed me out.

On rare occasions my group had moments of rest and recreation. During one such interlude we went to a California beach. I was fatigued from over a year of fundraising and lack of sleep and could only sit on the sand in a daze unable to think. I stared at the ocean waves and felt the hot sun beating down.

*

Even though scientists know little about the mystery of sleep, studies have been done on mental disturbances resulting from chronic sleep deprivation. Louis West, in a chapter titled *Psychopathology Produced by Sleep Deprivation,* describes how from ancient times prisoners in various situations were deprived of sleep so that their captors might coerce confessions from them. He states that with sleep deprivation "clouding of consciousness" lowers resistance to suggestion and subsequent manipulation causing difficulties in perceiving reality and disintegration of personality.

Fundraising for the cult day after day with four or five hours rest at night, month after month, contributed to the debilitation of my mind. West says that hallucinations often become a part of the altered state and contribute to "confusion and disorientation." The sleep-deprived individual's personality becomes unstable and, gradually, shows features resembling those of schizophrenia.

*

There was never enough money; the church always wanted more. From California we headed east, working across the country until we arrived in Omaha. There I received word that my father in Iowa was going to remarry. My parents having been divorced a few years earlier, he was now asking if I would come home for his wedding. It did not matter to me that he had found someone new but he clearly expected me to come home. And with the church's help I reluctantly bought a bus ticket.

*

"Turn that down!"

Once again on a school night the TV was the focal point of an argument. The apartment's livingroom was small as were the nearby bedrooms so I couldn't escape the noise. After my parents' divorce I lived for a time with my mother and younger brother.

Monday night football brought cheering fans, Howard Cosell and beer commercials full-blast into our home. I had been trying to do my homework and had been reading a book by Alan Watts in my room after supper but soon gave up for lack of concentration. After Scott refused to turn down the set I did it myself.

"How inane. What's wrong with you? Are you hard of hearing?"

"Just leave!" Scott yelled.

He got up off the Lazy Boy and increased the volume.

"This is my home too! You should be more considerate!" I said. "You're not the boss!"

Scott went to the kitchen and in a few seconds stood in front of me holding a steak knife inches from my chest.

"I'll kill you!" he screamed and added a string of profanities.

I stared at him and backed away. Mom was at the grocery store and not due back for a while. Bonnie, now in college, was living on her own. It was clear Scott's hatred had reached a new level and he seemed ready to make good his threat. This was not the first time he had displayed violent behavior. My father said no one could control him.

I inched toward the door.

"You're crazy!" I said and walked out into the building's hallway, stopping at the top of the stairway. Scott followed and before I knew what was happening he dropped the knife and shoved me down the flight of stairs. As I fell I struck my head on the banister and banged my arms while trying to catch my balance. I felt something break.

From the landing I looked up to see Scott laughing, his arms folded across his chest. He stooped down and picked up the knife.

"You ugly witch. Get out of here!"

Not knowing where to turn I walked out onto the ice-covered parking lot and headed toward the hospital two miles across town. Once there I found it deserted; it was after business hours. I walked to the cafeteria which was closed and curled up on the floor by locked doors. I had thought the hospital a place where people are taken care of and I wanted someone to take care of me.

No one came. Not a security guard. No medical personnel. After an hour or so I returned home, hoping my mother's presence would provide safety. The next day I went to school as usual but made plans to move in with my father and Stewart on the west side.

The first day back in Iowa City I attended the wedding and reception then gathered with relatives at my father's house. As the sun was setting I went outside and sat on the front lawn which gave a prickly sensation from having been recently mowed. I did this to escape my relatives' probing. I felt disconnected and conversing with them was an awkward struggle.

Just then Stewart came out and sat beside me. With classical good looks and a quick mind he was someone I admired but had not really gotten to know during childhood. Now in his twenties he was attending college and working full-time, living on his own.

My dad lived in a tidy modern neighborhood. Stewart and I watched children playing catch in a yard and riding bikes up and down the street.

"What are you majoring in?" I asked.

"History."

He seemed uncomfortable, looking around as though searching for words. Then he looked directly at me.

"Marcia, where have you been? What have you been doing in the Unification Church? How do you spend your time?"

Feeling secretive about my involvement I wanted to say as little as possible. I refused to answer his questions and looked away.

"You know this church is a cult, don't you?" he asked. "They have brainwashed you. You shouldn't go back!"

I wondered why my brother was telling me this and thought he had it all wrong.

"No, that isn't true. The church is not a cult and I'm not brainwashed. I *AM* going back!"

Stewart tore off a tuft of grass and threw it down.

"Listen Marcia, you don't know what you're doing. This could ruin your life. This cult is dangerous."

I thought that someday I could marry Dietrich. I thought that I must be loyal to Mr. Yamikama and the True Parents.

"No, I want to be in the church. I don't belong in Iowa. Nobody cares about me here. I'm going back. I am leaving on the bus tomorrow."

I got up and went inside. The next morning amid the protests of relatives, I left for the bus station. I had no feelings for these people; I wanted to be with my real family.

My team leader had directed me to take the bus to Chicago where fundraising continued. The team had assembled there while I was in Iowa. When I arrived the leader met me at the station and took me to join the rest of the group. While we were still in the van he instructed me by saying that a powerful way of controlling the spirit world is to pray under a cold shower. This would subdue the physical body while freeing the spirit. I asked if God would respond more readily if I did this and would I receive more answers to prayers? He said yes to both. And it would make me stronger and give me energy.

I contemplated his words and resolved to give it a try. However, when I began this austere practice it did little to strengthen me; I remained tired. One day I was selling candles door to door at run-down tenement houses. At one point I felt I could not go on so I laid down on a dirty front stoop, curling up in the doorway. I wanted to rest and wished the work would end. My eyes closed. After a time as if through a fog I made out a voice calling to me.

"Are you alright? What are you doing here?"

I opened my eyes to see two police officers, one bent over me and tapping me on the shoulder.

"Are you sick?"

Once again officers were apprehending me.

"Hey, this is a dangerous neighborhood, you shouldn't be here alone."

I struggled to my feet.

"I'm okay...just resting. I'm selling candles for the Unification Church."

"Come with us; we're taking you to the station."

One of the men took my arm and escorted me to the car. I did not argue but meekly complied. They told me they were not putting me in jail. They were merely concerned for my welfare and wanted me to phone my parents.

The station, in an afternoon lull, was nearly empty and quiet. A man in plain clothes watched me from behind his desk as I reluctantly dialed the number, unsure of what to say. Since it was Saturday chances were my father would be home. After several rings he answered.

"Hello, Dad?"

"Yes?" His voice, alarmed.

"This is Marcia; I'm at a police station in Chicago. They wanted me to call home."

"What are you doing there? Are you in jail? Are you in trouble?"

"No, no, I'm not in jail. I'm fine, just sort of tired. I'm going to call the center where I've been staying and have someone pick me up."

"Marcia, you should come home! That church is a cult and you should leave immediately!"

"No, Dad, I'm not coming home. And besides, I don't have any money. You don't need to worry about me. I'm going to hang up now…good-bye, Dad."

I hung up the phone.

My team leader picked me up in a half hour. Pulling away from the station he informed me that I would be sent back to New York the next day. I was done with fundraising, at least for now.

At last. Maybe soon I could get some rest.

CHAPTER 4

Back in New York I went to yet another training session at Belvedere. Most of the time we attended lectures given by Moon. When fundraising, I had sold products to a disinterested public and often met with rebuff. This humiliation wore away my self-respect and I soon lost it all. But even as this happened I was unaware of how I had deteriorated; I did not realize why I felt so badly. I only knew that I had to keep going, following orders and completing assigned tasks. By this time any doubt or resistance on my part had been destroyed. Moon's view of the world defined reality. Because of these various factors my mind was nearing collapse.

*

The church was a totalitarian regime built upon and, maintained by, what I later learned was spiritual fascism, a term Richard Delgado [a legal spokesman for the anti-cult movement] states was applied by leaders of established or traditional religious groups to describe the Unification Church's members lack of freedom of thought and choice. In my weakened physical and mental state, Moon's doctrine became imprinted on my mind. He gained power over me; I became someone he could manipulate for his own purposes. Throughout the year of training and fundraising I had started to lose my integrity and what dignity I had was destroyed.

*

When the session at Belvedere ended I was assigned to a new small group of women of American and Asian background, a new leader and a team mother. For almost two years we worked the northeastern part of the country, witnessing and fundraising. Every six months or so we had more training at Belvedere or gathered with thousands of others for rallies and addresses by Moon. My memories of this period are faint. I continued to be physically exhausted and even though I was part of a group, I was without friendship. Finally, in March 1976, my group arrived at the York Hotel, a New York City high-rise and Moon's latest real estate acquisition which had been converted into a gigantic church center.

Standing in front of the elevators in this hotel's lackluster lobby with dozens of others, I looked about for any familiar faces—hopefully, Dietrich or Mr. Yamikama—but to no avail. My group went first to a sleeping room on an upper level. After getting settled we began attending lectures and meals on the main floor.

Older men taught the Divine Principle and, as always during gatherings, we prayed and sang. For over three years I had had little privacy and now I felt overwhelmed by the pressure of constant group activities. One day I came to a breaking point, decided I had to be alone, and defiantly went in search of solitude.

Wandering about, I took an elevator to an upper floor and there found an empty room. It had a lock on the door which I resolved to keep securely fastened. There was a bathroom with a tub but except for a small wooden desk and chair, no furniture. The coarse, rusty-brown carpet was worn thin. The walls and ceiling were equally drab, marbled by cracks and without color. A window partially covered with dusty blinds gave a view of another high-rise across the street where I saw people busy in their offices.

I decided to stop going to lectures and instead, stayed in this room to pray, meditate, and study Moon's literature. Having been unable to find companions during my time in the church I now turned to God for fellowship through prayer. What I lacked socially I now sought through a connection to a higher power. However, I still concluded my prayers with "In the name of the True Parents."

Throughout the next few days I sat on the floor saying a mantra over and over. For this kind of meditation I had been taught to select a phrase from the Bible. Engaged in this practice, I lost track of the time of day and the day of the week. Without a clock I often went to the diningroom for meals only to find it empty, the tables without food. Missing meals was distressing; I became famished and went looking for food in the hotel.

On one occasion when searching the hallways I found a storage room full of fundraising candy. I helped myself to Baby Ruth bars and Junior Mints, eating these confections to the point of becoming dizzy but, at the same time, easing my hunger. I was already malnourished and such sugary meals did little to provide necessary nutrients.

One day after I had missed yet another meal, I went to the hotel lobby and approached several members, asking them for money so that I might go to a nearby McDonald's. All declined. I then waited several hours until dinner was served. My meal consumption became sporadic.

I had been living in the room for several days when, one afternoon, there was a knock on the door.

"Who is it?" I asked, standing close to the wooden frame.

A young man answered.

"Let me in, Marcia. I've come to talk to you."

He would not give his name.

"No!....Who are you?"

I was sure a leader had sent him to investigate my desertion of the group and to try to talk me into returning. But also, I feared sexual advances and kept the door locked to defend myself. He still refused to state his identity.

"Open the door."

"You can't come in. I don't want to talk to you—go away!"

This type of exchange continued for a few minutes before the unknown person gave up and left. I was greatly relieved and went back to my meditation sitting cross-legged on the floor. The area outside my room was rarely visited so it remained quiet except for outdoor street sounds—frequent police and ambulance sirens—which pierced the air of the metropolitan jungle known as Manhattan.

*

"I love you...."
A whispered voice gently spoke into my left ear. After that I sensed movement of something going around the back of my head to my right ear.
"I love you...."
Another soft whisper. My prayer trailed off as I became distracted by the voice. It started quietly and then crescendoed, continuing from outside my head, rushing faster and faster, back and forth, speaking into my ears. My eyes slowly opened and staring at the wall in front of me, I listened. Something was communicating with me; I thought it was a spirit.

Intrigued, I sat and listened as the whispers became rasping and guttural voices, first one, then two, then several. Some were raucous males and some, screeching females, but other voices were sexless, brazen and metallic, as though coming from an otherworldly entity. Soon they became belligerent and commanding.

"Take off all your clothes! Run down the street!"
"Don't wear a stitch!"
I had enough sense not to obey this order and did not budge from my place on the floor.
"You're going to die! Don't fight it!"
And then, "Jump out the window!....Do it! What are you waiting for?"
Still, I refused.
"Bow down!"
"Satan's bride, that's you! You're going to hell!"
The evil onslaught was overwhelming. Immersed in another realm I crept out of my room in search of release and

started to walk through the hotel. Roaming the hallways the voices surrounded me and continued to bark out orders.

"Go east!"

"No—west!"

I aimlessly walked to a door, opened it, and went onto a balcony of the hotel ballroom. I chose a seat near the railing which overlooked the dance floor. The huge room was empty. I sat listening to voices that shrieked and whined, a hideous mixture of venomous threats and shrewd poetry and I felt submerged in a murky underworld. My vision seemed cloudy as though I was looking through a brown mist. The light in the room was dim.

I was not able to think. Instead, I accepted the notion that disembodied voices were talking to me and I felt obligated to listen.

"There is no God!....No way out!"

"Serve me! The desert has many delights!

"Give up!"

"Six hours to go, Geronimo!"

"It's all hopeless, hopeless…meet me there."

After a while, tired of the nonsense and yet afraid, I left the ballroom and hotel, further compelled to walk. A brisk wind blew through my hair as I went through the front door onto the street.

"Your end is near…kill yourself!"

The voices howled through the wind as they brushed across my head and into my ears.

"You're lost… you'll never find your way… lost… lost…."

For no apparent reason I headed toward Grand Central Station. After several blocks I arrived and went inside. I sat on a bench amongst bag ladies and homeless men. A shabbily dressed woman clinging to a shopping cart containing her possessions was beside me. She turned to face me and with a kerchief tied below her chin opened her mouth, her lips not moving. A shrill grating voice came out but seemed not to be her own.

"You belong to the devil! Kill yourself! Maybe I'll kill you first! I'll cut your throat, hang you from a noose. Your end is near…you are going to die! There is no escape from the abyss!"

The hostile voice continued to spew hatred and obscenities with such a grinding tone it seemed to lacerate my ears. As it did so the woman sat stiffly and remained expressionless, and even though her mouth was open, her lips did not form the words. It made my skin crawl. She appeared to be possessed by an evil spirit that was speaking through her. Shaken, I abruptly got up and left.

I walked out of the terminal on unsteady legs and headed toward Rockefeller Center.

"Come, you can trust me!"

"No rules! No rules!"

It looked like it would rain soon. Only a few people were milling around or sitting on benches. It was a gathering place for all sorts. Again, without conscious awareness of why I was doing something, I approached a man who looked like a mafia gangster, the kind I had seen in the movies who wore a suit coat over a black shirt and tie. He was not the typical candidate for witnessing but for some unknown reason I wanted to prove to him that he didn't scare me.

"Grab the ax!"

"Off with her head!"

I went up to this stranger and mentioning the Unification Church I invited him to a lecture. His eyes glared a silent rebuttal as he reached for something inside his coat. Sensing danger, I turned away and headed back to the York Hotel.

"Proclaim the darkness!"

"There is no escape!"

Menacing voices laughed derisively.

*

In later years I tried to find out how my cult experience may have contributed to mental disturbance. Many believe the Unification Church brainwashes its members and when I found Joost A. M. Meerloo's *THE RAPE OF THE MIND: The Psychology of Thought Control, Menticide, and Brainwashing*, I discovered that a link may exist between what happens when one is brainwashed and the development of mental breakdown.

Much of my cult experience confirmed Meerloo's account of mind control methods: the constant ideological lectures of a totalitarian leader, separation from society and its culture, lack of privacy, continuous planned activities, encouragement of child-like dependence on the leader, and sleep and food deprivation which can lead to altered states of consciousness and, eventually, psychosis. The characteristics of psychosis listed in the *DIAGNOSTIC and STATISTICAL MANUAL of MENTAL DISORDERS [DSM-IV]* are: delusions, hallucinations, disorganized speech and behavior, confusion or perplexity, and a lack of emotional response to environment.

As my own psychosis progressed I was further deprived of sleep, for the voices did not relent even at night. In this way, my mental state became self-perpetuating and contact with reality further decreased. West, the author of the study on mental disturbances resulting from chronic sleep deprivation, believes that environmental factors play a strong part in alteration of mental states. And along with the psychopathology comes a physiological state of the body reflecting and contributing to the altered condition of the mind.

*

I had only been back in my room a short while when there was another knock on my door.

"Who is it?" I asked.

"It is Shoko. I've come to see you. Are you sick?"

Shoko was a Japanese woman in a high position and a constant companion and translator for Mr. Yamikama. I hadn't seen either one for months. Shoko was stunningly beautiful with dark oval eyes, rounded cheekbones, and black hair closely cut to frame her face. I was in awe of her.

Not feeling threatened I opened the door and she walked in. We sat on the floor and she peeled a grapefruit, setting the sections on a napkin.

"You are sick, Marcia. Eat this fruit. You also need to have give and take."

"What do you mean by 'give and take'?" I asked.

"You need to talk with people. If you spend more time doing that you will feel better," she said.

"Your chains will never be broken!" a voice interjected.

"Enthroned... enthroned below — serve me!" said another.

I put a piece of grapefruit in my mouth and, finding it bitter, was disappointed she had not brought sugar along.

Shoko didn't know I had been hearing voices. I now suspect a leader had sent her to evaluate my mental condition to see if I could be of further use to the church. At one point, I decided to confide in her.

"I hear voices constantly."

Searching her face for any kind of reaction, I found none. She carried on in a monotone.

"There are other people in the church who hear voices too," she said as she smoothed the napkin with her fingers.

"Recently, a young man jumped from an upper floor window to his death while obeying a voice. Also, Mrs. Lee, an older Korean member, hears voices. She lives in a house near Belvedere and stays there all the time listening to them. They are spirits, Marcia. You are open to the spiritual world. You've had a spiritual awakening."

I accepted her explanation without question or emotion. My years in the church had seemed to create a numbness or dullness in feeling that made emotional response difficult.

"Also," she continued, "someone recently fell down a broken elevator shaft and was killed. You need to be careful."

I shuttered at the thought of someone finding a broken body at the bottom of a shaft.

"What kind of work are you going to do now for Father? Just ignore the voices—they are not important. You should have goals, work to do. You are young."

"Twenty-two, I'm twenty-two years old."

"You must get involved again in Father's work. You just can't stay here alone."

Shoko's demand that I have goals for my life reminded me of an earlier time, a time when I had pursued meaningful work.

*

One day in sociology class we saw a film about Third World hunger. It showed babies in rows of cribs that caretakers were trying to feed, yet there wasn't enough food and the babies cried. The narrator said that many people suffer from malnutrition and millions die of starvation every year. I was horrified and left the room in a state of shock. My sheltered upbringing had not prepared me for such a harsh reality as this.

As the other students filed out I saw them laughing, joking, and carrying on in usual fashion. I thought they hadn't understood what they'd seen, or if they did, just hadn't cared. What was more likely was that they felt uncomfortable and didn't know how to deal with those feelings. Maybe laughter was a way to hide their discomfort.

I thought of going to see the pastor of my church, Reverend Windale. I needed a sympathetic ear and someone who would validate my own concern for the Third World. In a vague sense I had become aware of a desire to do something useful with my life and now sought the pastor's reassurance. Maybe, just maybe, I could break out of my oppressive home environment by striving for something better.

As was typical of American families in the 50's my family attended church every Sunday. According to my mother's records, at two years of age, all through the week I would eagerly ask my mother if it was the day to go to church. But as a teen, I lost interest in such things. Attending church with my family I would arrive at Sunday school with incomplete lessons and would struggle to pay attention in class. While in the services I was preoccupied with thoughts about what I was wearing, how my hair looked, and whether someone I had a crush on at school might phone. The emotional and intellectual depth of sin and salvation barely took root, if at all. But now, after seeing the sociology film, I instinctively felt Reverend Windale could help.

On impulse, I left school and walked downtown to my Lutheran church. Once there the secretary allowed me to approach Reverend Windale's door. I knocked, after which I heard a muffled, "Come in."

The Reverend's small office was crowded with bookshelves, his desk, and two black vinyl and metal chairs facing it. He was seated with one hand holding a pipe; its aroma filled the room.

It didn't occur to me that I might be doing anything out of the ordinary—leaving school to discuss Third World poverty. I thought that if I needed to talk to someone I should do just that.

"Hello, Marcia. What brings you here?" he asked and smiled warmly.

"There are so many people hungry and starving in other parts of the world! So much suffering—people are dying!" I blurted out.

Framed by a sunlit window Reverend Windale appeared rather startled but nodded in acknowledgment. He was in his 60's with white hair and his bearded face had a rough, outdoorsman look. He was known for his love of hunting.

With what appeared to be solemn understanding he said, "Yes, the condition is grave. Is that what brings you here? You look upset. Are you alright? Sit down."

I seated myself and placed my purse and books on the floor.

"I saw a film in class—aren't there organizations that help the Third World? Maybe when I get out of school I can do something."

"The Peace Corps. They do a lot of their work in Africa and other Third World areas," Reverend Windale said. "Also religious organizations run relief programs to give aid. I wish I could send you into the world as a Joan of Arc to help the poor, but I can't do that. So, you're looking at your options. You'll graduate soon?"

"Yes, this June. I think I'll look into the Peace Corps."

We spoke a while longer. I never mentioned the problems at home or that I was being treated by a therapist. Reverend Windale was a compassionate man, one who had allowed a troubled girl to interrupt his busy afternoon to discuss what she felt was important.

Later, I went to the library and learned that Joan of Arc, born Jeanne la Pucelle, was a devout Catholic in the 1400's who led the French army in an attempt to free her country from English rule. She heard voices, rebelled against religious authorities, and was burned at the stake.

Toward the end of my senior year I met with a school guidance counselor to discuss my plans. But since she saw that I had had difficulty meeting the challenges of school work she discouraged me. Her disapproval was disappointing and further lowered my own estimation of my abilities. Without goals for my life the future looked bleak. I felt only pessimism and hopelessness.

Joan of Arc's voices had helped her to lead an army to fight against English oppression, but my voices were the oppression itself from which I sought escape, a way out. Unlike Joan of Arc my voices were not leading me; instead, they clearly intended harm.

*

Shoko told me that Father was planning a massive rally and speech in Madison Square Garden and gave me directions on how to get there from the hotel. Then she said good-bye and left. I was sorry when Shoko got up to leave. It had been a privilege to spend time with her. Her parting words did not indicate any future action, but I intended to continue living where I was. In the following days and nights the voices continued to engulf me in a hellish nightmare.

Shoko had said Father was inviting the people of New York—via pamphlets and witnessing—to attend his rally. I decided to go. So on the appointed afternoon I joined thousands flooding into the stands of Madison Spare Garden. There I listened to an impassioned speech but as though from a distance and without being able to concentrate. He spoke for over an hour before the crowd dispersed. Leaving the Garden, I felt lost, alone, and cut off, even though people were all around.

"There are no answers...trust no one!"

"All is in vain—give up!"

"Surrender to me!"

Voices shrieked and wailed.

I started to be gripped by fear. What was I supposed to do now? I couldn't pray because of the voices. I wondered why Shoko hadn't offered to help me. People had been jumping from hotel windows, falling down elevator shafts. My chest tightened with anxiety and I hurried back to my room. Once there I was surprised to find my possessions gone: a change of clothes, the book *MASTER SPEAKS*, toiletries, bath towel, paper and pen. Alarmed, I searched for someone to ask what had happened. I found my former team leader as he was passing through the lobby.

"Where are my things? Do you know who took the clothes out of the room I was staying in?" I asked him, my voice at a high pitch.

His cool response revealed annoyance.

"They were taken to the midtown center. You'll find them in a storage room in the attic."

"Why? What on earth for?" I asked.

The leader kept looking away as though not wanting to look me in the eye. He would not answer and started to step away.

"I'm busy. Now, stop bothering me."

He turned his back and was gone before I could catch my breath. Anxious to get my things I hurried several blocks to the center. But on the way I grew afraid. I heard snarling and growling as though German Shepherds were chasing me and closing in. Inside the center doors I still did not feel safe. The place was active with people working on church business or functions.

I approached a secretary sitting at a desk and asked where the attic storage room was. She said she would show me and got up, leading the way. We went up several flights of stairs to a dimly lit hallway and halfway down she opened a small door.

"Here's the storage room."

I gasped and my hands went to the sides of my head.

"Oh, my—

Tears welled up in my eyes. I saw huge piles of discarded clothes, suitcases, purses, torn blankets, hairbrushes, toothbrushes, books and other objects. The disarray covered the entire floor; to find my possessions in such chaos would be impossible.

Voices taunted with gales of laughter.

"You dirty whore! Shame on you!"

"You're guilty—to the gallows!"

"I have work to do," the secretary said before turning to go.

I knelt down and wept. Everything I had was now gone. The church had taken what little I had owned in the world and discarded it, leaving me with nothing. I had devoted my life to this organization and it repaid me with this. Its betrayal devastated me; I was utterly alone.

I got up, wiped the tears from my face and sought a way out of the building. Now invisible giants followed me. I sensed and heard their footsteps. I wondered what they might want with me. The cacophonous voices now occasionally mentioned my physical father's name.

"This is the Tim Murphy Show! The Tim Murphy Show!"

"No matter what you do, you can't get rid of us!"

"We are controlling you—puppet on a string!"

I passed through an unoccupied room that had drafting tables on which were dozens of black and white photos. Glancing through them I recognized many leaders: Shoko, Mr. Yamikama and others. They posed comically, holding pieces of fruit in absurd ways, their faces contorted in laughter and jest. The photos must have been party scenes with people mocking and jeering for the camera. This was not meant for me to see. I quickly left the room and continued down to the main floor not knowing where to go from there.

Suddenly, two women appeared at my sides taking my arms and escorting me out the door onto the sidewalk. I protested as they continued to force me down the street.

"What were you doing at this center? Come with us!" one said.

"Hey, leave me alone! What's going on?" I protested.

Our struggle on the crowded sidewalk drew the attention of passing police officers.

"What's the trouble here?" one asked as he took a step toward us.

"Tell them to let me go!" I pleaded as the women gripped my arms even tighter.

"She's crazy! We're taking care of her. She's a member of our church. There isn't any problem. We can handle—

"I'm *NOT* crazy! It isn't true…help me!" I cried out to the officers.

Siding with the women the policemen allowed them to take me away. I was mortified.

In a few minutes we arrived outside the York Hotel. There they had me get into the back seat of an old Buick and the driver told me we were going to a place in Irvington called Jacob House not far from Belvedere. As we headed north on the dark highway the atonality of a devil's chorus clamored from the car windows and rose up from around its wheels outside.

"Hey, whore! This car is about to crash!"

"There is no hope!"

"Jesus saves?! Not on your life! There is no Christ!"

"You are lost forever—you are in the darkness!"

"Your end is near! Meet defeat!"

The persecution became ferocious as surging demonic voices became a thunderous roar.

"NOTHING MATTERS!!....THERE IS NO MEANING!!"

"YOU WILL BURN IN HELL!! YOU BELONG TO SATAN!!"

"YOU ARE GOING TO DIE!....TO DIE…TO DIE!!!"

I crouched on the dirty floor behind the driver and covered my ears, but I dared not close my eyes.

"THERE IS NO ESCAPE!!"

"GIVE IN AND CHECK OUT!!....YOU LOSE!!"

Never before had the voices struck such fear in my heart. There was something very real about them. During the whole trip they surrounded the car and flowed through it. At one point I started to pray.

"Oh, God, please help me! Save me, Lord!....Help me!"

"GOD CAN'T SAVE YOU!!! GOD DOESN'T EXIST!!! THERE IS NO GOD!!! NO ONE HEARS YOU!!!....FOOL!!!"

On they raged. I became hysterical, praying louder and sobbing all the way to the estate. Finally, we arrived at Jacob House and the voices subsided to their usual conversational tone. Terror-crazed, I went in the front door behind the driver and met the leader who took me to a back room. He gave me a sleeping bag, comb, toothbrush and a tube of toothpaste. He led me upstairs to sleeping quarters provided for a dozen other women and myself. I lay down, light-headed and confused. Moments later the room was filled with women who had just completed evening prayers. Some laughed and giggled, enjoying each other's company.

The church found little value in members who could not raise funds or witness. And now I was in such a position. It was still providing shelter and food, at least for the time being. My existence was marginal; I fought to hang on. It felt as though some force or forces were trying to destroy me. I was fighting for my life.

CHAPTER 5

I'm so tired; I don't have any energy.

I crawled out of my sleeping bag at 4:45am. The stuffy room was crowded with women most of whom I had never met, but there were a few familiar faces. One was Tracy, pretty and confident. She spoke for the second time

"Up, everyone! Pledge morning. Be at the Prayer Room by five!"

Every Sunday members stood in rows and recited the loyalty pledge to the True Parents. During this morning's recitation I only felt semi-awake because of the early hour. When the ritual was completed I went downstairs to the coffee room, an annex of the dining area with windows that provided a view of the backyard garden. I made a cup of instant Folgers, adding several spoons of sugar and creamer to help jump-start my day. This was the first of many cups I would consume over the next several hours. The voices had continued throughout the night except when fitful sleep provided some peace. This being the first morning at the center I didn't know what to do; then Chad, the director, approached me.

"For the rest of the summer I want you to do housework," he said. He had dark curly hair, a slender build, and was an American in his mid-twenties. He seemed to enjoy telling people what to do.

"Simple enough," I replied and then I began to clean the kitchen, washing dishes and sweeping the floor. The rhythmic strokes of the broom across the linoleum felt soothing and as people came and went I moved around them calmly. The kitchen was a gathering place for those who had nothing to do and where they often fixed themselves meals of plain white rice. Though they spoke with one another I had more important things to do; I had to listen to other voices.

"TWA Flight 41 from Dallas and St. Louis has arrived. Passengers may be met at gate C-4," a smooth, disembodied female voice announced from nowhere. I kept up my work.

"United—curbside! Customer service please," she continued, trailing off in a whine.

The laundry room was through a doorway next to the kitchen. It was here that I did my favorite chores, washing and drying clothes. I enjoyed making things clean and neat. However, because of the voices, this task became a challenge. The running water and mechanical noises from the washing machine spoke, as did the hot air dryer tossing clothes.

"Loser! Failure! You can't do anything right! Never could, never will!"

"I don't know the reason....Do *YOU* know the reason?"

"Lies are as sweet as honey! Laws are to be broken!"

When the voices were critical it hurt; I couldn't ignore them. Mornings, when I took a shower, water from the nozzle spoke. And brushing my teeth, the water falling from the faucet spoke just as it did when I washed dishes at the kitchen sink. Once, as I walked down a window-lined corridor, I saw on the carpet several crickets hopping about.

"I love you, Marcia....I love you!" each one chirped cheerfully.

I paused to admire them thinking they were such nice, friendly crickets.

*

One cloudy day after several weeks at Jacob House a group of us were taken on an outing. Chad drove us to Barrytown in Dutchess County north of New York City where a seminary that Moon had purchased from a Catholic organization was located. It appeared to date from the early twentieth century with its old stone walls. As the car wound along a tree-bordered lane and approached the front entrance, Shoko came into view walking gracefully in private reverie along the hillside. The woods surrounding the compound provided a pleasant place to stroll unhindered by church responsibilities. She was the most elegant woman I had ever known. I was pleased to see her and knew that Mr. Yamikama and, possibly Moon, must be there also.

"Father said we are supposed to tour the seminary and then go to the sanctuary for prayers; after that he will join us." Chad said.

The building spread over several acres. The rooms were dank and drafty like an ancient castle and they had little furniture. After our walk through the building we entered the huge sanctuary where mass had once been held for Catholic men in training to be priests. I looked up at the high ceiling and then to tall windows from which light filtered onto the place where an altar had been. Everyone kneeled on the stone floor, said individual prayers, then sat and waited for Moon. Soon he walked in with Mr. Yamikama, Shoko, and Colonel Pak. Following close behind was a young man carrying a large cardboard box. Father seemed pleased. As usual, he spoke Korean and Colonel Pak interpreted.

"I have Bibles for you! I will autograph them and then you will possess the Messiah's signature! How fortunate you are!"

We were thrilled and took turns standing in front of him while he opened black, leather-bound Bibles and signed his name on the inside cover. In addition to the English version of his name, he wrote in Korean. I had never owned a Bible; this was certainly a treasure. When the signing had ended Father had words of instruction.

"Until our mission with the Christian church is over we must quote the Bible and use it to explain the Divine Principle. After we receive the inheritance of the Christian church we will be free to teach without the Bible. But even if we do not inherit the Christian church, we will succeed. The Unification Church has become so precious in the sight of God that he will say, 'Satan, so you want the world? Okay, take the world for it is crumbling anyway. Do you want a church? Take Christianity. But you cannot touch the Unification Church!'

"Father is the Adam who will restore the failure of Jesus. Jesus never achieved a thousandth of what Father has done. In Jesus' two years and eight months of public ministry he didn't even establish the national foundation. Now Father established a foundation of worldwide power that is unprecedented in history.

"Jesus is not even in the kingdom of heaven. I saw him in a vision and he is in Paradise. Did Jesus come in order to liberate the world? Did he fulfill his mission? No, he did not. Since his mission was not completed he was not victorious and did not liberate the world and is not loved as a son by God. This is the path of the Unification Church today. I am the Christ; we will be victorious!"

Everyone started clapping and Father smiled broadly. Then he had everyone take a walk in the nearby woods, after which, my group returned to Irvington.

Had I opened my Bible to the beginning three books of the gospel I would have read a warning given by Jesus Himself, that many will come in His name claiming that they are the Messiah. Jesus said that we should not be deceived or follow them.

Back at the house along with cleaning I helped with a day care center that occupied a large upper room. Mass marriages arranged by Moon produced children who were often separated from their parents soon after birth. Husbands and wives were also separated and sent on missions to different parts of the country or world. This center had few toys and no children's books. The children did not receive adequate nutrition so both their mental and physical growth was stunted. Their medical and dental care was based on emergencies. I found child care monotonous and escaped by walking out.

Since I was always tired, often during the day I tried to nap. But just as often as I put my head down, vicious and demonic voices threatened me from the floor as if coming up from an underworld, the very bowels of the earth.

"I'll destroy you!"

"Do what I say or be damned!"

"Into the river of death! You must die!"
"No rest—you will never find rest!"
"Burn in HELL!"

Voices yelled a torrent of obscenities and blasphemy. I would shake with fear and, not knowing where to turn, force myself to get up and find something to do.

*

Every few weeks Moon gave lectures at Belvedere to gatherings of several hundred members from the New York area. The car taking my group there wove in and out of traffic and as it did so the motors and mufflers of cars, trucks, and motorcycles blasted at me.

"I aaam thirrrrrsssty forrrrr yyourrr bblooood!"

"Lovvvve mmmeeee, loooovvve mmmeee; I willl ggiiivvve yyoooou poooooowwwweeeerrrr....!"

I reasoned that satellites must have beamed voices to these vehicles. But I didn't know what it all meant. Entering the lecture hall I saw a woman vacuuming and the loud whirr of the cleaner directed hostile accusations towards me.

"YOU F—ING MACHINE!!"

"YOU ARE A F—ING MACHINE!!"

The cleaner continued hurling filthy insults and accused me of performing degrading sexual acts. I was offended and relieved when the woman was finished with vacuuming. But since it was a hot day someone turned on a box fan which sent me messages until the room filled with people and Moon began to speak. He spoke for two hours; then we sang, prayed, and finally left.

When I wasn't cleaning or napping I read church books, something that had been enjoyable for me. But now this became difficult for as I read the words I heard them out loud.

"Jesus was supposed to find a woman to be his wife. Had he done so he would have brought her up through instruction and spiritual discipline to his level, which was perfection. Then he and his wife would have produced perfect children and thus begun the kingdom of heaven on earth. But Jesus failed to accomplish his mission...."

Soon I gave up reading all together but this increased my sense of isolation and depression. Authors were no longer my companions. With this and frequent rejection by those I lived with, my loneliness reached new depths.

My situation seemed bleak. Constant voices made it hard for me to think my own thoughts. I didn't have any hope for the future; I didn't anticipate that my situation would improve nor did I know the meaning of my suffering, if there was any. I was losing the strength to go on.

After three months at the center my will was almost completely broken and I stopped doing chores. The daily routine now consisted of rising for coffee and breakfast, then napping until lunch. After lunch I'd sleep again and then get up for dinner. I only desired to sleep, to escape the nightmare.

One day I was trying to rest and was having difficulty because I heard evil spirit music, the sound I imagine George Bernard Shaw was referring to as "the brandy of the damned" or music from hell.

All afternoon thick clouds had accumulated outside into an ominous darkness, until finally, a thunderstorm arose. Rain fell in torrents, saturating the earth. Lightning flashed with loud cracks, so much so, I cringed in fear, startled with each new strike. Far and near, thunder rumbled.

Regardless of the potential danger I got up from the floor and walked to the open bay windows overlooking the garden. Surrounding the garden were rocky cliffs with overhanging trees and shrubs growing from their crevices. The heavy downpour soon became a voice, a voice from unfathomable depths—nonhuman, extraordinary, and otherworldly.

"BELIEVE IN JESUS CHRIST AND YOU'LL BE SAVED!!"

In astonishment and awe I slowly backed away from the window, water dripping from its ledge. I went to my sleeping bag and sat down. Even though I didn't know what to make of this message I felt a glimmer of hope as faint memories from childhood floated up and I was comforted. To understand what had happened seemed difficult. The experience was ineffable, yet images came to my mind: Jesus, the strong Shepherd with a lamb in His arms, held close to His heart; Jesus, hanging from a cross with nails through hands and feet, tortured in body and soul; Jesus, the resurrected, conqueror of death, redeemer of souls, Savior of the lost.

A few years before when I had sung the Lord's Prayer at the boulder I had asked God to deliver me from evil. Though at the time I thought little of it, this may have been a life-saving act of faith. Now, without aid from any source, God alone reached down to deliver me from my desperate situation. This God, the One I had depended on from birth, would never forsake me regardless of circumstance. But would I heed this answer to my prayer?

As the days progressed other things happened. Sometimes at night, when retiring for the day in bed, the voices made me laugh and feel better if only for a moment. And once at bedtime when the crickets in the yard were chirping, they chorused into a celestial song of angels, a mosaic of harmonious voices—the invisible world's missa solemnis.

While walking in the garden bees flew from blossom to blossom buzzing messages. The purring of a neighbor's cat also became a voice. Quite often, if I spent time in the kitchen cooking or watching others fix meals, the flame from a burner spoke. I would listen and then become distracted by and drawn to the people present.

From every person there seemed to emanate a field of consciousness that intersected and merged with my own. A melding took place of my spirit and theirs. And then, sometimes, the joining went beyond persons in my immediate surroundings and I felt at one with the entire universe or so I thought. At these times there were no boundaries between myself and others. If I admired someone I didn't mind the fusion; but if a bad character was near I felt my spirit becoming contaminated or polluted. Then I tried to get away.

*

"When I enter a room I can feel the emotions experienced by people who have been there immediately before. I sense them spiritually."

Dietrich had said this a few years prior, claiming to have supernatural powers. I remember being intrigued; I thought he must have been telepathic. I began to suspect such special powers in other church members as well.

One day I was summoned from the upstairs room to the foyer of the house. Mr. Nishika, the first Asian leader I had met in New York, had been visiting the center and asked to see me. As I walked down the wide staircase to the entrance way I braced myself for an assault on my mind. Standing in front of him I stared at the floor and suddenly became unaware of my surroundings. I focused only on his voice.

"Marcia, look at me! Look into my eyes....Hey! I'm up here!" he said sternly as he placed his hand under my chin.

But I refused and he appeared frustrated. He walked a few paces, came back, and put his hands on his hips. I cowered beneath his glare.

"What do you do at the center now? Do you work?"

Though I took naps all day I tried to convince him that I continued to be productive. Still, I averted my eyes.

"Yes, I do housework...I vacuum, wash dishes, sweep the kitchen floor. I work very hard!"

Mr. Nishika seemed to accept what I said but still he pressed on.

"Marcia, I said *LOOK* at me. I demand that you look into my eyes! *NOW*!!"

I never gave in and he finally left. I was certain that had I looked into his eyes he would have gained telepathic control over my mind. All my thoughts would have come under his dominion and he would have possessed my spirit. I had to resist at all costs.

Summer passed and then in September I received a call from my sister. This was surprising because in the past the church had not allowed phone conversations with relatives. Chad had me take the call in the kitchen. It was early evening.

"Marcia, this is Bonnie. Are you alright? I haven't seen you for so long! Jonathan, my new husband—you haven't met him—he and I are flying to Europe but we are stopping off in New York and we'd like to visit you. Is that okay? Why don't you tell me where you are. Where is the center?"

I did not want her to come or see the condition I was in.

"Bonnie, I'm fine. The church wouldn't want you to visit. You'd better not."

"Are you sure?" her voice pleaded. "We'll be in New York for a few days. We just want to drop in for a visit. I really miss you!"

She seemed a million miles away, her small voice on the line weak and fearful. But I was in another world and it was no place for my family so I turned her down.

"No, you shouldn't come. You'd better not. I'm sorry…good-bye."

I hung up.

But that call stirred something within me, a notion that something was amiss. My sister's care and concern touched my heart when it was becoming clear that the church would not help me. I thought about how hard I had worked at fundraising and how the leaders were always being chauffeured around in limousines and Mercedes. They lived in luxurious mansions with servants to wait on them while members like me had only the barest necessities. So I decided to go home, if only for a visit.

I wouldn't stay long.

CHAPTER 6

"United Flight 583 to Chicago. At this time all confirmed passengers should be on board through gate B-1. Immediate departure—2pm. Final call."

Once again I was at LaGuardia, only this time I was headed home via Chicago. The church had Chad buy me a ticket and drop me off. After an afternoon of travel I arrived at the Iowa terminal and from there used the airport van service to go to my father's house. When I knocked on the back door he was surprised to see me. After letting me in he phoned my mother to tell her I was there. Then he, his wife, and I went to the livingroom.

After exchanging some small talk my father asked: "How long are you planning to stay?"

"Just a couple of days."

They looked disappointed and tried to persuade me to leave the organization.

"You can live with us," my father said.

"You could get a temporary job at the academic testing center," his wife said. "They hire on a regular basis."

I just looked at them without comment.

The next day we went to visit my mother. She had stayed home from work to see me. She was an experienced counselor but now abandoned her professional manner in an effort to reach her daughter.

"Marcia, we've been so worried about you. The Unification Church is a cult. They brainwash people! That Moon has become rich off his followers' fundraising. Please don't go back—you shouldn't go back! Stay here with us and get a real job!"

I felt confused.

"No, I'm going back; I don't want to stay in Iowa."

Voices interjected with tittering and gales of laughter mocking my words.

"*NOOOO, I'M GOING BACKKKKK...I DON'T WANT TO STAY IN....IOWA!!!*"

My parents and I had trouble communicating. After some arguing we gave up trying. I walked out the door and around the neighborhood looking for relief from the conflict and clamoring voices. I was distraught to the point of nausea and a headache. I tried to think of a way out.

I thought it would be awful to live at home again. I didn't feel they loved me though I know now they really did. I thought they were critical and demanding but I know now they just wanted the best for me. But since I had memories of how I had felt threatened at home and became suicidal I thought I should leave again.

When I got back to the house I told my father, "I'll need a ride to the airport tomorrow. Will you take me?"

He nodded and said he would.

The next morning my father and I picked up my mother and then on the way through town we pulled into the parking lot of my childhood church. The back door swung open and I was surprised to see Pastor Windale as he got in beside me.

"We're taking a drive," my father said. "We're going to Minneapolis; it will take about six hours."

He had lied to me; we were not going to the airport, but I accepted the turn of events in silence. Once we arrived at our destination I saw that it was a house in a blue-collar neighborhood with lots of barking dogs. Everyone got out of the car and my mother took my arm, escorting me up the sidewalk. My footsteps spoke in staccato bursts.

"This—is—the—end!"

"This—is—the—beginning!"

After my father pushed the buzzer a tall, heavy-set woman in her early forties opened the door. She greeted us, took a drag on a cigarette then let us in. A young man behind her quickly stepped aside.

"Hi, I'm Cathy."

The others gave their names as well but I remained silent.

"Let's all go to the basement," she said cheerily.

Downstairs we found ourselves in a room with cement block walls, tiled floor, and a tangled ceiling of wooden beams, plumbing, electrical wires and cobwebs. I thought I detected cockroaches scurrying in a flash into crevices. A bare light bulb was suspended from the center. There were five folding chairs in a row facing a single one. Cathy had me sit on the lone chair and everyone else sat looking at me. With this, the onslaught began.

"*Soooo,* Marcia, you're a *MOONIE!*" Cathy began in a high-pitched friendly but false tone. "How long have you been in the Unification Church?!"

"A few years," I mumbled.

Others stirred in their seats.

"Have you been happy there?" she asked, her voice growing louder.

"It's alright."

"Which center have you been staying at? Where is it located?"

"It's in New York."

"Your parents want you to live at home and get a job—do you think you could do that?"

"No...no. I don't want to do that."

Cathy told my parents and Pastor Windale to go upstairs but asked Tom, the young man, to stay. She told me to move my chair into a corner. Tom placed two chairs right in front of mine and we sat facing each other amidst a cloud of smoke from Cathy's cigarette. Without warning she shouted.

"YOU STUPID B—! DUMB MOONIE! THE UNIFICATION CHURCH IS A CULT AND YOU'RE

MOON'S DUPE! YOU'RE ONLY FIT FOR THE SEWER! VILE—THAT'S WHAT YOU ARE!"

Swinging her hand to her mouth she sucked greedily on the cancer stick, her chest heaving. She exhaled with such force that the smoke stung my eyes. I turned away.

"LOOK AT ME!" she yelled. " I'M TALKING TO YOU!!"

I recoiled from these attacks. After a smirk she continued at the top of her lungs.

"WHORE! PROSTITUTE! YOU FILTHY SLUT!....." and on she cursed, letting loose a string of profanities—this fire-breathing ghoul.

I was confused. Whore? Prostitute? Hadn't I remained celibate and spent my time fundraising, cleaning, and praying? I wondered why she hated me; how had I offended her?

She mocked my look of discomfort, contorting her mouth and squinting her eyes.

"YOU F—ING B—! RANK PIECE OF GARBAGE! YOU THINK MOON IS THE MESSIAH? WELL, HE'S NOT! AND THE DIVINE PRINCIPLE IS RUBBISH TOO!"

I was incredulous and agonizing over what to say, remained silent. I wondered how my parents could allow this to go on for I knew they heard everything from upstairs. It was then that I felt the widening gulf between us would be difficult to mend.

But Cathy had an agenda.

"I'LL TELL YOU WHAT YOU ARE, YOU FILTHY SWINE! MOON'S ZOMBIE! A MINDLESS ROBOT! YOUR HEAD IS EMPTY AND HE'S CONTROLLING YOU! DENOUNCE THE CULT! THERE ARE NO TRUE PARENTS—FOOL!!"

Tears fell down my cheeks and I wanted to tell her to stop yelling but couldn't get the words out. I glanced at Tom beside her. His eyes were wide and his mouth hung open.

"YOU F—ING WHORE! D— YOU TO HELL! YOU SHOULDN'T PRAY TO MOON! HE'S NOT THE LORD OF THE SECOND ADVENT!!"

She paused only to light another cigarette.

"YOU ARE NOT GOING BACK, B—! TRY IT AND WE'LL LOCK YOU UP IN A MENTAL INSTITUTION! SO DON'T EVEN THINK ABOUT IT!...."

Suspended between the realities of the cult, the voices, and the outside world, my fragmented mind did not know which way to turn. But regardless of the direction the question remained as to whether I could sustain that choice. I was drawn to Moon's organization by the people I had grown fond of even though I had begun to question their integrity. I had to escape the mad, surreal world I was now a part of, but I saw no way out.

When Cathy's voice grew hoarse she stopped and ordered me to follow her up to the kitchen. She walked straight to the refrigerator, took out a Bud and popped it open. In my distress I went up to Pastor Windale sitting at the kitchen table. He reached out and put his arm around my waist.

"It'll be alright; things will be okay," he said in a low voice.

But it wasn't alright. From the conversation I learned that Cathy was a deprogrammer. I later found that deprogrammers came in two versions: the calm college graduates who present documented evidence of corrupt cult practices and those of Cathy's sort who apply an emotional shock treatment intended to jar a cult member back into reality.

"What are you going to do with Marcia now?" my mother asked.

I felt a captive.

"During the next two weeks," Cathy said, "I'm keeping her in the house except for a trip to the optician to get her some new glasses. I'll let her watch TV and read magazines or books I've got here."

Throughout the evening the bizarre scenario continued to unfold. Before my parents and the pastor left my father had everyone sit in the basement again. He explained that he was to sing in a talent show at the school where he was a librarian. We were fortunate, he said, to have a sneak preview. Standing in front he cleared his throat and began.

The shadow of your smile when you have gone will color all my dreams and light the dawn....Look into my eyes my love and see all the lovely things you are to me....Now when I remember spring, all the joys that love can bring, I will be remembering the shadow of your smile....

*

For the next several days I did very little. I wasn't interested in talking with Tom. Cathy told me that he had left a cult called The Children of God. His parents were having him stay with her for a month. I decided to keep my distance.

One afternoon when I was left alone in the livingroom I dashed out the front door and down onto the street. I then crossed to another and slowed to a walk, all the while glancing over my shoulder.

"This is the final boarding call for TWA Flight 637 through St. Louis and Dallas! All passengers must be on board the butterfly at this time....Fly away...fly, fly away!....Final boarding call! Gate C-4!"

I realized I didn't know the way to the airport. Eventually, I reached a Seven-Eleven where I sat on the curb of the store's parking lot and watched the customers come and go.

"Sacrifice to me—you repulsive worm!"

"There's no refuge, no escape!"

Snarls, shrieks, and howls.

"Sharpen the blade!"

Suddenly, a helicopter flew overhead. Fearing it might be the police I ducked into the store. But after a few minutes I thought the coast clear and went out to sit on the curb again. As I was pondering what to do a serious looking middle-aged man approached me holding out money.

"Here's twenty dollars," he said gruffly as he tried to hand it to me.

"No thank you!" I snapped, fearing he thought me a prostitute.

Jumping up, I walked out of the parking lot. I realized I had nowhere to go and, being penniless, had few options.

Slowly, I made my way back to Cathy's and walked in the door. She was sitting on the couch and didn't appear alarmed so I quietly took a seat in front of the TV.

At the end of two weeks my parents came and took me back to Iowa where I stayed at my father's house.

*

"I'm taking you to see a psychiatrist," my mother said over the phone. "Be ready at nine-thirty tomorrow morning; I'll be coming by to pick you up."

It was now October 1976 and I had been back in Iowa City a couple of days. I didn't know what to expect from seeing this physician and was wary. As my mother and I walked down the drab hallway of the psychiatric hospital I pictured myself lying within its walls convulsing from electric shock treatments and other horrors. Built in 1921, the building had originally been named the Iowa State Psychopathic Hospital, the first of its kind west of the Mississippi. In the 1970's the name had been changed to convey something less derogatory and stigmatizing though I thought the building still appeared spooky. We stopped outside a door with a sign on the wall next to it saying, "Dr. Hayes."

The secretary directed me through a nearby door into the psychiatrist's office. As I went in the door closed behind me. Dr. Hayes stood up from behind a large wooden desk. He was a tall, thin man with fine sandy hair and wire-rim glasses. He walked over, introduced himself, and shook my hand. He had a sophisticated manner though understated, a gentleman of the old world when civilities mattered and were clearly expected. Though he appeared to be in his forties he seemed older spiritually, a little tired and resigned to his profession's demands. At the time of our meeting I was unaware of the importance this would have for my future, the lifeline it represented.

As we sat down I noticed a foxtail fern on the corner of his desk. Staring at its tender leaves I began explaining my unhappiness at being there.

"I don't trust you. I don't believe in psychiatry—it was not my idea to come and speak to you."

Unfazed, Dr. Hayes began to ask questions.

"I spoke with your mother briefly. She said you just left the Unification Church which you were a part of for a few years. Is that correct?"

"Yes, but I'm still interested in it."

"We'll eat you alive!"

"Rip you to pieces!"

"Do you feel upset about your present situation?" he asked.

"Yes, I feel my parents are trying to control me. They betrayed me—they took me against my will to a deprogrammer. She was mean."

My tone became louder and abrasive.

"I left Moon's church because I was threatened. My parents said they'll lock me up in a mental institution if I try to go back."

Dr. Hayes nodded his head in understanding but remained reserved. After a moment of silence he questioned me again.

"What do you want to do now?"

The voices whined and wailed. Perplexed, I groped for what to say next.

"I want…I want to be left alone. I want an apartment of my own where I can do some art work and study. I want to study the Unification Church but not rejoin it."

"Do you think you'd like to talk with someone, a therapist or me over the next several weeks?"

"On the wings of the vulture! Harlot!"

I became adamant.

"I have no desire to talk to anyone, I don't need that. I'm not feeling stressed. The only reason I can't get along with my parents is because they're always telling me what to do. I don't really want to hurt them though."

"Sinking! No foothold!—you're sinking into the miry depths!"

"Foodwaters...engulfing you! Into the depths—swallowing you up!"

We talked for almost an hour and all the while I never mentioned the voices. In responding to Dr. Hayes' questions I sometimes made contradictory statements. When he pointed this out I easily rationalized away the inconsistencies.

Finally, he said, "That's all for today," and the session ended. I got up and left. After I was gone Dr. Hayes wrote the following in his notes:

> I have no experience in this area but judge that the deprogramming is incomplete. I also judge that, in her present state, this young woman is highly susceptible to outside influence and that perhaps for some time her behavior will be erratic as first one attitude comes to the fore and is replaced by another. One might predict a degree of instability, interference with goal-directed behavior, a lack of long-term aims and, periodically, a good deal of inner distress. There is no diagnosis that seems appropriate. There is no current sign of depression, no hint of psychosis. The picture she presents is nevertheless distinctly abnormal, whatever we might call it....

After my mother took me to my father's house the two of them went back to Dr. Hayes' office to discuss his evaluation and decide on future plans. He advised that I have supervision and therapy but saw no indication for hospitalization or medication. He told them I had no desire to continue seeing him and would probably resist therapy. My parents disagreed about what to do next.

For the next several days they tried to convince me to apply for jobs. But I was too distraught. Instead, I had my father drop me off at the University campus on his way to work mornings. I walked amongst the students longing to fit in but not knowing how. My father had given me some spending money so I spent hours in restaurants drinking coffee and sodas. Then one late afternoon I phoned Dietrich. He was living in Los Angeles and attending college. He bought a plane ticket for me so, once again, I left Iowa for the cult—this time heading west to California.

CHAPTER 7

Dietrich lived in a modern apartment complex complete with a community building that had laundry facilities and an exercise room. He was attending classes at UCLA, paid for by the Unification Church. I realized with annoyance that my fundraising had financed his schooling.

"You're not going to be here very long," Dietrich said. "I'll be driving you to Santa Barbara tomorrow afternoon. You can sleep in the bedroom tonight—I'll take the couch. Right now I have to go to class then the library to finish a paper."

"I can take care of myself."

"Here is a key; lock up when you go out."

Along with the key he handed me a twenty.

"Take this and buy some food for tonight's dinner. The store is down the block just past the gas station."

He left.

"Go to the store! Go to the store! Chicken and eggs…eggs and chicken…the store and more!"

That evening after Dietrich and I ate my simple meal I decided to go to bed because he said little and preferred to ignore me. I became discouraged from trying to get him to talk. He was distant and aloof; his coldness was unnerving. I started to get nervous, so much so, that I secretly took a knife from the kitchen and placed it under my pillow for protection. My feelings for him were an odd mixture of admiration and fear.

In the morning I discovered the knife was gone. I searched everywhere in the bedroom and could not find it. I entered the livingroom fully dressed having worn my clothes all night.

"Did you take the knife?" I asked Dietrich who sat on the couch eating blueberry muffins and drinking coffee while watching the *Today Show*.

Swallowing his food he turned to me and started to laugh loudly.

"What knife? I haven't seen a knife!"

He continued to laugh and I stared at him for a minute then let the subject drop. That morning he drove me in his red 240-Z sports car to a center about an hour north of LA. We pulled up to a dusty old ranch-style motel that had been purchased by Moon. Dietrich explained that they did fundraising and little else. I was disappointed but that was not important to him.

"When will I see you again?" I asked as we sat in the car.

No response; he looked straight ahead. I thought he had a regal profile. My visit with him had been much too short. Even though the night before I had been afraid I now fully trusted him again.

"Dietrich, will you come back soon?"

"Give me the key," he said turning and holding out his palm.

"What—?"

"The key to my apartment."

"No, tell me—when are you coming back?"

"Give me the key!"

I reached into my purse, found the key and held it tightly. His face grew red, like he was ready to explode.

"Give me the key!!" he shouted.

Reluctantly, I slapped it onto his hand.

"Now, get out!"

I got out and slammed the door. His tires skidded as he tore away from the curb. The center's director was expecting me and had me room with some of the other women. Wasting no time, the next day the director told me to go with the group to sell flowers in a mall parking lot. I refused.

"I'm never doing that again."

"If you're not going to work then you'll have to go," he said. "I'll put you on a bus tomorrow for New York. We don't want you here! You're leaving!"

Dietrich didn't want me, now this. But Father, Mr. Yamikama, and Shoko were in New York. I would be more at home there. That afternoon I wandered around the center not knowing what to do. At one point I came across a bathroom scale, stepped on it and weighed myself. I couldn't believe the needle.

While involved in the Unification Church I had neglected my appearance and over-ate. Before the voices I had been so focused on my spiritual life that I had not noticed how I looked. And after they started I cared even less. I thought I needed to exercise to lose weight and so I decided to go for a walk.

It was sunny and leaving the center I went through a small business district to a residential neighborhood with streets lined with parked cars. Voices, gruff and throaty, croaked and snarled.

"You will burn in the fire...never extinguished!"

"It's what you deserve, b—!"

"I'll bathe my feet in your blood!"

Voices added degrading and humiliating insults. But even as all this was going on something else caught my attention. A filmy, gray cloud in the shape of a human figure had appeared in the front seat of a stationary car. It looked to me like an old lady sitting behind the steering wheel. After a few seconds it vanished.

I continued walking, until suddenly, a snarling stray dog ran up. Of medium size and black fur, it barred its teeth prepared to attack. Standing still, I glared at the animal resolving to use telepathic power to gain control. It glared back. Then slowly, only a few feet away, it stopped, turned around, and retreated. I hurried back to the center.

The next day with just my purse and a small bag I boarded a Greyhound on which I spent three days and nights traveling from warm California to snowy New York. I walked to the York Hotel and got there just as Moon and his entourage were arriving. They sped past to the ballroom and I followed joining hundreds already assembled there. Moon proceeded to give a speech.

"I will give you a new vision and a new spiritual power! Salvation of the world is our primary goal. Sacrifice yourself to save humanity and the world. I am God's instrument….Be very aggressive to achieve victory! Be adventurous and very bold! Do everything with strong conviction. Never stop until you have finished a task—don't stop half-way. Fulfill and accomplish all that I ask! We are the international family! We are beautiful in God's eyes…."

As I listened my eyes were drawn to the balcony. There I met the penetrating stare of Mr. Nishika. Months ago at Jacob House he had attempted to engage me in conversation but I felt he had tried to exert control over my thoughts. Now a mysterious power seemed to connect his dark eyes and mine. I located the stairway, went up, and stood beside him.

"Hi, Mr. Nishika."

He wore a long black trench coat. Smiling, he took a step towards me.

"Hello, how are you, Marcia? I haven't seen you for such a long time! Did you just get back to New York? It's good to see you again."

He grasped my hand and lowered his voice.

"Are you tired? Why don't you come upstairs to my room?"

I abruptly pulled my hand away and took several steps back. My eyes scanned the crowd below and I found Chad, my former leader from Irvington. I immediately went down and told him that I wanted to return to Jacob House. After the rally ended he allowed me to return there with a vanload of other members.

*

Memories of the next several months are dim. I felt my situation was hopeless and that I had little to live for. I was slowed by constant fatigue and a haunting sadness. I was nagged by the thought that I had made a mistake in returning to New York. As before, my efforts to make friends were rebuffed. Even though I lived with dozens of others, few gave me their attention. Often upon approaching one or another to converse they would say, "I don't have time for this!" or "Get back to work!"

For the rest of the winter I cleaned house. My days consisted mainly of work interspersed with rest periods. Thoughts of my grandmother came to mind—her high standards in cleanliness—as I scrubbed floors, faucets, and dishes. So I wrote to her about my work though not mentioning who was giving the instructions.

"Clean—clean those floors!"

"Shine those faucets! Hey—you missed a spot!"

"Lazy! Who do you think you are anyway?!"

"Get down on those knees and scrub! You heard me! Quit stalling!"

*

Spring arrived and I did less work. I spent time carrying plants outside to give them sunshine then bringing them back in. To my disappointment some died, but for a while this activity absorbed my attention.

Jacob House, surrounded by a lawn and woods, had a narrow lane leading to a minor highway that if taken long enough would bring one to Moon's estate. His multi-million dollar mansion was positioned on a hill a quarter mile from the entrance gate and fence consisting of black metal bars spiked at the top. One cloudy day I decided to go for a walk and headed down the lane from Jacob House through a gray mist. After a mile or so around a few curves and up a hill, with an occasional car passing by, I reached the edge of the estate. Standing in tall weeds I peered through the fence, keeping my distance from the armed guards. I felt empty, yet yearned for a glimpse of the master.

After several minutes I heard the hum of an approaching motor and the sound of rocks crunching under tires and I turned to see a shiny black limousine. As it slowly passed a dark figure leaned forward from the backseat and a tan Asian face appeared in the side window, eyes searching.

Father!

His eyes met mine but soon registered disappointment. His mouth became a frown and he swiftly drew back. I stared, feeling small, disenchanted. The limousine turned into the drive-way, paused by the guard, then went through the opened gate.

He was gone—that was the last time I ever saw him.

*

Summer came and went. I could no longer think clearly and chores became even more difficult. I struggled as best I could then finally gave up. I had lost the ability to cope. I wanted help.

One afternoon I went to Chad who was sitting in the kitchen drinking a cup of ginseng tea. As I stood limply in front of him the window rattled from a gust of wind.

"I can't do this."

"What? What are you talking about—can't do what?"

He put down his cup.

"I have to go home…please help me, I need to go home."

Through half-closed eyes I thought I saw a smile flicker across his face.

"Fine! You're quite useless around here these days. We'll let you go! I'll take you to the airport as soon as it can be arranged. If Dietrich had not been your spiritual father things would not have been so easy for you. High position has its advantages, doesn't it? Start getting your things together!"

I turned and walked away.

Howling laughter.

"Copping out, slut?! You'll burn!"

"You're a loser—everyone hates you!"

"Give in, check out!"

"It's a wrap!!"

CHAPTER 8

"Mom, I hear voices."

We sat in front of a picture window as snow fell softly outside. I had been home for a month trying to get along as best I could following the directions of my parents who wanted me to find employment. It was December of 1977 and I was twenty-three years old.

"I'll kill you!" a voice shouted.

"Now you're done for—it's all over for you! You b—! Death for you!"

It blasted a string of profanities.

My mother sat bolt upright, a look of panic on her face.

"How long has this been going on? What are they saying?"

Then without giving me time to answer she said with alarm, "You need to see a psychiatrist! I didn't know you were that sick!"

She hurried to the phone on the wall saying, "I'll call the clinic right away and set up an appointment with Dr. Hayes. He's the psychiatrist you saw a while back."

My mother had always been a woman of few words and even now, after hearing this alarming news, said little more. She may have been in shock because of the severity of my illness.

With her back turned to me she held the receiver to her ear. I saw her head nod after she explained to Dr. Hayes that I was sick and she asked to meet with him that afternoon. My appointment was the next day.

As I walked into his office Dr. Hayes stood, then walked over and greeted me with an out-stretched hand. He wore a navy cardigan sweater over a white shirt with a dark gray tie. I was absorbed in confusing emotions and felt detached, so initially, my seeing him again had little effect.

"Hello, Marcia. *How are you?*"

Dr. Hayes' voice registered deep concern but feeling mistrustful and avoiding eye contact I murmured, "Alright."

My thoughts were interrupted by the evil force.

"Venom of snakes—drink the poison!"

"You are a god! You don't need anyone!"

"There is no truth...."

After we were seated I looked down and noticed my winter boots were covered with snow. I felt guilty about the little puddles I would leave on the linoleum tiles. Dr. Hayes asked about my life since the last appointment. My gaze still at my feet, I told him about my trip to California and New York in the year since I had seen him last. Then I decided to confide in him.

"I hear...voices," I said in a subdued tone.

"Traitor!!" came a loud accusation.

"I'll suffocate you! I'll silence you!"

I felt terrified.

Without emotion he asked gently, "How long has this been going on?"

"I've heard them for about a year and a half," I said. "It's been a nightmare! Also, men have been trying to control my mind!"

Dr. Hayes seemed interested and replied, "In what way do you mean?"

I glanced up as I spoke.

"Their spirits become fused with mine. Their minds are like clouds that come over me and oppress me. They manipulate me with their thoughts—like I'm a puppet."

Still preferring to keep some distance I again avoided looking at Dr. Hayes. Instead, my gaze now fell upon the white lawn visible through a small window above his left shoulder.

Then, reaching to the floor, I nervously rearranged my purse, leaning it against the leg of my chair.

"After coming back to live with my mother and younger brother I found a job as a kitchen helper at the hospital but the people who worked there were mean and we quarreled. The supervisor let me go after a week but it wasn't my fault. They were hard to get along with. No one was friendly and I was hearing voices—they always make a commotion unless I'm talking. There's something about my own voice that drowns them out."

A feeling of relief came over me because, finally, someone was listening to me—not making demands or arguing. Not scolding or shouting. Just listening. For much of my life I had felt as though what happened to me didn't matter. But now I began to feel differently, that someone cared.

"Sometimes, when I read a book or a magazine, the words become voices I hear out loud. In California I saw a ghost in a car—an elderly lady sitting behind the steering wheel. I've been very tired; it's hard to sleep at night."

It suddenly struck me of how bizarre all this must sound and I became frightened of being locked up in the psychiatric hospital where I was sure I would be tortured. But even though I was afraid of being mentally ill I still wanted to know this psychiatrist's view of what I experienced.

Dr. Hayes questioned me again.

"What did the people in the Unification Church think of the voices? What did they tell you?"

I looked him directly in the eye.

"They said I had an awakening to the spiritual world. I don't know what it all means. What do you think?"

"I believe you are ill," Dr. Hayes said, "and I recommend that you take medication."

The voices yelled loud curses.

For the next several minutes we continued to talk about the voices. What did they say? Was I frightened of them? Then we discussed what kinds of things I could do between now and the next time we would meet. In all, the appointment lasted about fifty minutes and toward the end he handed me a prescription.

"Please return next week at the same time."

I told Dr. Hayes I would start taking the medication that night. After I left he did as he had the year before and entered a note in my record:

> At this time, Marcia's mother describes her as seeming at times to be far away, emotionally distant, aimless....It appears to me that she has little interest in things....Marcia describes hearing voices which are sometimes pleasant, sometimes arouse her curiosity, but are sometimes accusatory. She finds that her concentration is poor, that she is listless. She seeks identification with and direction from people such as her mother.

After some partial success the next several years would be filled with a litany of ineffective treatments.

*

I had just finished lunch one day when I heard rapid knocking. When I opened the door there stood my beautiful sister with suitcase in hand and tears streaming down her face.

"Oh, Marcia!!" she cried and rushed in to hug me. "Are you okay?"

I had never received such affection from Bonnie. She had always kept her distance. I hugged her back but said nothing. That afternoon my grandmother in Davenport invited us for a visit. My grandparents hadn't seen Bonnie for a while. She lived in Oklahoma and I had been away for more than three years. The next day my mother drove us east on Interstate 80.

"There's no hope!! A death warrant's out on your life!"

"Give in! Extinguish the flame....The moth will die!"

We arrived at my grandparents' house, one built in the 30's and located near a city park with a greenhouse and duck pond. I followed my sister in through the back door. I envied her long blond hair, slender figure, and stylish clothes. As we greeted my grandparents I hoped they would be pleased to see us but they were reserved and cheerless. Perhaps their hard life had robbed them of joy. Ill health and harsh economic realities had taken their toll.

Following German ancestry my grandparents' home was spotless and in perfect order. To my surprise I noticed that once in the house an amazing thing happened. The loud belligerent voices disappeared and were replaced by soft soothing ones. They voices were sweet and gentle. *Baby angels!* I thought. We seated ourselves in the livingroom and there beneath fluttering wings I heard messages that filled me with peace.

"It's alright....It's alright now."

"Don't worry...you are safe, you are safe."

"Don't cry, Marcia...don't cry anymore."

"There, there...don't dismay. We'll help you...we love you."

Distracted by the angels I paid little attention to my surroundings. I thought I should tell Dr. Hayes about them.

After dinner my grandmother, mother, sister, and I washed, dried, and put away the dishes. Then it was time to go. When I left the house the celestial voices remained behind and I was plunged once again into the realm of darkness.

CHAPTER 9

I began to look forward to talking with the psychiatrist. I arrived for my next appointment full of hope. Maybe he could help. After initial greetings he asked, "How have you been doing?"

I straightened my sweater and fastened the top button. My eyes fell on his desk where I noticed folders and books neatly stacked.

"I've been talking more and my thoughts are clearer. I believe this is an improvement so I would like to keep taking the medication."

"No one hears you—witch!"

"We'll destroy you with fire and sword! We'll scatter your bones!"

Blaring obscenities, again, spewed forth.

"Have you noticed any side effects from the medication?"

"No."

"Then I'd like you to double the dose."

I agreed to do as he directed then started to share with him what had been on my mind.

"I keep thinking about the past—I can't think of a future. It's like I really don't have a future. And anyway, I'm scared about what could happen."

Sitting stiffly in my chair I waited for Dr. Hayes to comment. When he remained silent I continued.

"What is the meaning in life? Can I really trust anyone?"

Looking thoughtful, Dr. Hayes opened his mouth to speak but before he could I spoke again, changing the subject.

"I used to think that the voices I heard from animals and machines were beamed from satellites. They were forces of good and evil battling with one another. But now I'm not sure. I don't see how this communication could happen. Several times it came through cats."

I looked away. Frustrated at trying to figure out what was going on I was beginning to think Dr. Hayes didn't know either.

Voices mocked in syrupy false pity.

"Weep and mourn…mourn and weep."

"I would like to get rid of the voices if it is not normal to hear them. They are still constant and make it hard for me to concentrate."

"I understand that must be difficult," Dr. Hayes said.

For the rest of the session we discussed my ability to sleep, my eating habits, and what I did to occupy myself. For the most part, I was dysfunctional in all of these areas yet had been successful in grooming and occasional reading. Also, I had gone jogging to try to work off the effects of overeating. When our time ended Dr. Hayes said he would see me again in a week.

> I feel there is little doubt about a diagnosis of schizophrenia here, and I note that a cousin was diagnosed as having schizophrenia and committed suicide….Marcia is fearful of her impulses and she so readily identifies with others that the boundaries of her identity are blurred. She seems preoccupied and raises any number of unanswerable, basic questions about life….

According to the Catholic Encyclopedia there are accounts of medical treatment for the insane from ancient times in places around the world such as Egypt and Greece. Historical evidence of treatment dates to the Christian era. Around the fourth century many people with mental illness were cared for in Christian monasteries. In England, as early as 900 A.D., herbal prescriptions were thought to benefit melancholia, hallucinations, mental vacancy, dementia, and folly.

By the thirteenth century Bedlam, a London hospital, had a separate department for people with mental illness as did many other general hospitals. Another English asylum near the Tower of London was established by Robert Denton in 1371. He wanted to provide for priests and laymen who would get into a "frenzy" or lose their memory. About this time there is also a record of a place for "mad people" in Rome.

Early German institutions were established between 1100 and 1300. Spain established several asylums in the 1400's and had a reputation for the best care in Europe through the early 1800's. During the 1600's the French established colonies for people with mental illness. These consisted of country places where they could work when able, but when they became too ill they were taken back to a central asylum.

The first mental institution in the United States was established in Williamsburg, Virginia in 1773 at a time when a more humane approach was being taken toward people with mental illness. This slowly replaced the brutality common to early asylums. In 1817 the Friends' Asylum in Frankfort, Pennsylvania promoted and practiced "gentle, intelligent care for the insane." But even into the twentieth century mechanical restraints such as chains, manacles, and other severe methods were used. The advent of psychiatric drugs in the 1950's brought a "biological revolution" that changed the way mental illness was viewed and how patients were treated. Medications helped many people with mental illness to be able to lead productive lives.

In modern times most mental institutions are state-run and an open-door policy allows freedom of movement not only within the institution but coming and going as well. Now those who are able see psychiatrists on an out-patient basis, visiting clinics for therapy and medication adjustment while living in sheltered half-way houses in the community, with family or in their own homes.

*

The following week's session began with a discussion of practical activities, plans, and goals. I had been told of an opportunity to move into a half-way house, called the Women's Residence, in June. This place provided a supervised setting and counseling aimed toward independent living and employment. I had been invited to see the house and then asked to decide if that was what I wanted to do. I told Dr. Hayes about my recent visit there.

"The director said I will be helping with the cleaning and cooking. The other residents look awfully sick; maybe I can help them somehow. I'd also like to make new friends."

"What other kinds of things would you like to do?"

I thought for a moment then said, "I would like to get a part-time job and later full-time. But first I want to lose fifteen pounds and go to a hair stylist. I'd feel better about myself then."

As we discussed these externals I sensed that deeper needs would not be met so I explained more about my problems.

"I feel restless and nervous and have a hard time sleeping—it's like I'm kind of scared."

"How long has this been going on?" Dr. Hayes asked.

"For over a year," I said.

"We'll make you sleep in the dust!"

"Coward—turn back!"

"You're a disgrace!"

As I sat across from Dr. Hayes I looked at him and thought how alien he seemed. He had had such a different life from mine. I thought he probably came from a secure home, one that gave him emotional stability so that he might study then work hard as a physician and professor. He had admirable accomplishments and had achieved the respect of important people. I thought that compared with him I was a total failure and my life, a total loss.

"You're from another planet!" I blurted out.

Dr. Hayes appeared startled but managed to maintain his composure. Deciding not to pursue the matter he asked another question.

"How are the voices? Do you still hear them?"

"They are constant. I wonder where they are coming from—it's a mystery."

Dr. Hayes responded matter-of-factly to my questions of where the voices originated. He said they were hallucinations and that I was ill. He ended the session by saying, "I hope you will see improvement soon."

I left that day with a dim hope that I might. However, I was still saddened by the powerful emotional turmoil generated by my years in the Unification Church. No one asked me what had happened back then, what my experience had been. I was just supposed to go forward, ignore the memories, and forget the trauma. I was not to concern myself with the past but begin a new life regardless of how sterile or superficial it felt.

*

I discovered that the University Recreation Building had an indoor track where jogging was allowed. In the dead of winter and needing something to do, this seemed like an option. Even though most days I wanted to stay in bed I found exercise a diversion from the voices. So one afternoon I made the mile-long walk to the Rec Building. My mother had generously given me a pair of running shoes and I was anxious to try them out.

Walking up to the facility I passed through a large parking lot and there in front of the building were bushes full of sparrows. They were hopping about from branch to branch and fluttering their wings excitedly. But these were no ordinary birds!

"I love you, Marcia!!"

"I love you….I love you….!"

Dozens of tiny little birdie voices chirped in glee, repeating these words over and over. I was captivated. Their message of cheer lifted my spirits. After pausing to listen I went inside and started around the track. But my enthusiasm was short-lived. I was in bad shape and soon out of breath. So after only a few minutes, I left.

On the way back home I felt the cold air seep through my coat and I pulled my hat down over my ears. Suddenly, a car passed by full of teen-aged boys.

"Hey, ugly!"

"Pig!"

"Stupid b—!"

Howling laughter.

I looked away and hoped no one had noticed. Nearing my mother's block my eyes were drawn to the electrical wires strung along poles at the edge of the street. At regular intervals on the wires were red blinking lights used to divert planes. There was an airport nearby. Voices came from the wires and lights.

"Hhhhhuuuummmm…watch out!"

"Airplane coming...bombs away…direct hit!"

"Fffffoooorward mmmmaaarrch!…one, two, three…."

"Bbbbbaaatttle ssstttaations! Ffffuuulll sssspeeeed aaahhhead!"

"Mmmmaaaay ddddaaayyy! Mmmmaaayy dayyyy!"

I wanted to get out of the cold and soon reached my destination.

The following day I visited the hospital again for my appointment. Once inside Dr. Hayes' office I draped my winter coat over the back of my chair. Sitting down, I volunteered good news.

"Dr. Hayes, I noticed that when I am distracted or with people I enjoy I may not hear the voices which is an improvement. But I also welcome certain ones. Like when little birds talk to me. It makes me sad to think that if I get well I will have to leave the good voices behind. But most of the time they are horrible."

I lapsed into silence looking down at my hands. I thought that maybe my hopes were in vain. Perhaps he wouldn't be able to help and I would always suffer from this oppression.

Dr. Hayes encouraged me to say more.

"How are you getting along with your family?"

Immediately, I felt a rush of anger.

"I don't trust them. I don't feel good when I'm around them. I had a nice time at my grandparents' house but usually when I'm with my relatives we don't get along. During my sister's visit I felt better but it didn't last."

We discussed this situation for a while then I asked, "What is my diagnosis?"

"You have schizophrenia."

For a brief moment I held my breath then let it out.

"Do I have to have shock treatments?"

"No, you'll just take medication."

I was greatly relieved. We ended the session by discussing my plans to move into the Women's Residence whenever they had an opening. These practical steps toward improving my situation were acts of faith on my part. I wanted to comply; after all, these people were the experts and knew what was best. They were doing all they could.

Yet I wanted more. I wanted to know what had happened to me. I wanted to know the meaning of my suffering, the reason why I had gotten ill. All the external props would have little effect unless my innermost being could find the answers. Until then my soul would not be satisfied, my mind would not be healed.

CHAPTER 10

After leaving the cult for the last time I stopped praying. I had given up hope that God would help me and the voices continued to dominate my life. I was still enveloped in darkness, a spiritual black hole where any entering light disappeared into the void. And, as in my teen-age years, I now felt trapped living with my mother and Scott.

Her apartment was small and provided little privacy. We were not happy being together and this created an atmosphere of hostility. Like the time earlier in my life, daily quarrels once again escalated into emotional violence. Scott's aggression was still uncontrollable as it had been when we were younger. He had attacked me then and it was clear his disposition hadn't changed. I felt I needed justice; I needed an ally.

Finally, on a January morning in 1978, I felt so desperate that I asked my mother to take me to the psychiatric hospital to be admitted as an in-patient. There was little discussion. We packed a small suitcase and within an hour I found myself seated in a stark room with pale yellow walls and with an exam table in the middle. There was a place to view x-rays and a blood pressure cuff off to the side.

I waited for the resident who would determine whether I would be admitted to the hospital. Psychiatrists had different roles—I could only see Dr. Hayes as an out-patient and not while in the hospital. My mother spoke to the admitting doctor in another room. Finally, a man who appeared to be in his late twenties came in and sat down. He placed a notepad on his knee and reached into his breast pocket for a pen. I noticed an expensive watch on his wrist.

"Hello, Miss Murphy. I'm going to ask you a few questions. I understand you've been involved in a cult called the Unification Church and you've been hearing voices for about a year and a half. Why don't you tell me about that."

I told the resident about my activities. Then I explained, "I hear rain, animals, and machines talk. Sometimes they're funny, sometimes religious. But mostly, they're evil and frightening. They call me bad names—

Abruptly, I stopped because the humming of the fluorescent light had begun to speak.

"Have your own sweet way! Now you've done it!"

Looking up toward the voices I told the resident what was happening.

"I think the voice from the light and those coming through the walls, running water, and pipes are from a machine that is trying to control me."

He continued to take down notes and did not respond, so I continued.

"Last summer communists were hiding microphones to spy on me...."

"Do you know who our country's current president is?" the resident asked.

"Carter, I think."

"How is your appetite?"

It was funny he should ask; I was beginning to feel hungry and wished the interview would end so that I could get some food.

"Alright," I said.

But the resident wanted to know more.

"What kinds of things have you been doing with your time?"

"I'm usually so tired I just stay in bed and listen to the voices. Sometimes I go running on an indoor track. But there is something in the floor that pulls me down and makes it hard to run. Once in a while I'll watch TV. When the TV is off I have a feeling that there are people looking through it at me."

"Do you sleep well?"

"For a while I thought the voices were less at night but over the past few weeks they have become louder and more Satanic so I'm not able to get much sleep. I have to turn on the bedroom light because I'm so scared. I'm exhausted trying to figure out what is wrong with me."

The resident said little which left me feeling odd. After what seemed a long time he finished the interview with two last questions.

"Do you feel suicidal or like you want to kill someone else?"

"No, I don't."

After a brief physical exam the resident led me down the hall past vacant offices, up stairs, and through the locked doors of West Ward. He told me to take a seat in the dayroom, an area with a plain couch, comfortable chairs, and tables where patients congregated. There was a nonfunctioning dark brick fireplace, worn carpet, and bookcases and shelves with wrinkled magazines such as Readers' Digest, Ladies' Home Journal; various books, picture puzzles, and board games. On one side of the room long windows with locked screens (no bars) provided a view of the adjacent Health Science Library surrounded by trees.

Many patients sat in the dayroom doing nothing but staring vacantly. One was talking to himself. I looked closely at his face and an eerie feeling came over me as I noticed his eyes darting in different directions as though a desperate struggle were taking place behind them. Others spoke with staff or visitors. Many were unkempt with dirty hair and mismatched clothes. A woman with short permed hair, glasses, and a denim dress approached me and sat down. Though the physicians on the unit wore white coats, most of the other staff wore regular street clothes.

"Hi, Marcia, I'm Andrea. I'll be your nurse while you're here."

After shuffling some papers she fastened them to a clipboard and then, poised with pen in hand, asked in a sarcastic tone, "So! You hear *voices*?"

Taken aback, I mumbled, "Yyyyes….yes I do."

Frowning, she prodded further in what seemed to me apparent disbelief.

"What do they say?" she demanded.

Feeling threatened and intimidated by her coldness my mind went blank.

"I don't remember," I said looking away.

Andrea's tone softened.

"That's too bad you can't remember."

I thought *maybe it isn't*.

The nurse proceeded to ask questions like those of the resident. After a while I heard a clanging bell.

"It's lunch time. Come with me," Andrea said leading the way.

The dining area had a series of round tables seating four apiece. On each were platters of over-cooked beef patties, bowls of corn and syrupy fruit cocktail. We got drinks at the counter by a window through which I saw people in uniforms scrubbing pots and pans. Perspiration poured down their faces as clouds of steam rose from the sinks. I took the nearest chair and soon all the places were taken. I felt awkward but soon was just grateful for the meal.

After lunch Andrea brought me to a private room with a bed, small table and chair. On the way there we passed a large room with several beds near the nurses' station. The station had large glass windows on two sides and a split wooden door with a ledge from which medications were dispensed. It included built-in desks and a table in the center that held a round metal chart rack. During the day the area was crowded with staff bumping into one another: ward clerks, nursing assistants, RN's, medical students, residents, staff physicians, and others. It was here nurses and psychiatrists consulted with one another and made notes in the medical record about how patients had done during their shift.

Down the hall was the Quiet Room, the place for violent or hard to handle patients. One day as I walked past I caught a glimpse of what was inside. It had a linoleum floor with a drain in the middle. On the floor was a mattress covered with plastic and ruffled sheets. The door had a window for staff to look through and a huge skeleton key hung nearby. The room was not soundproof so screaming and yelling—common among the occupants—could be heard throughout the ward.

"You can't stay in your room during the day. The snack cart is brought out at 10am, 2 and 7pm in front of the diningroom. It has crackers, fruit, milk, cookies and other things," Andrea said crisply after which she turned and left.

"You will perish! No one will save you...."

"We have the perfect plan...."

Gurgling laughter.

*

The psychiatric hospital consisted of two wards, East and West, with about thirty patients each, both men and women. They were as young as eighteen but the majority were in their late twenties to age forty. Some had developed mental illness at a younger age but had been able to stay out of the hospital until later in life. The average stay was about a month. The patients were evaluated, treated, and if they needed long-term care were sent to a state institution.

Following a physical examination at admission patients were given their own clothes unless they were on "elopement precautions." Such precautions were taken if it was believed the patient might try to escape. When this happened the staff would try to find them or ask police to bring them back. Purses and other possessions were kept in the business office. And sharp things patients might use to hurt themselves or others were kept in a partitioned drawer and given out for temporary use.

Along with the examination tests were done: EKG (electrocardiogram), electrolytes, thyroid function tests, and if the patient was to have electric shock treatments, a chest x-ray.

Shock treatments were administered in the back of East Ward. In this room, besides the electrical stimulus generator, there was an emergency cart, suction machine, IV set-up, drug tray and respiratory equipment. Shock treatments were used to treat depression and catatonia when medications proved ineffective.

Nursing assistants woke patients at seven, breakfast was at eight, and medications were given out. There were group activities during the day such as bowling, volleyball, and trips to ice cream and donut shops. Also, patients went to therapy groups for problems like depression. Medications were given out again between nine and ten at night.

Patients were encouraged to be out of their rooms but some were too sleepy to comply, often a side effect caused by medication. Occasionally, in four-bed rooms, patients were allowed to sit on their beds and talk. The TV in the dayroom was turned off at 11:30pm on week nights and 12:30am on weekends.

There was a pay-telephone in a small locked room and patients had to have their own money for its use. They were monitored by staff for length and appropriateness of calls. When outsiders phoned they first had to call the nurses' station. Then the patient would be notified and take the call in the phone room.

*

Since I was only allowed on my bed at night I lay down on the couch in the dayroom and there withdrew into myself. With closed eyes I listened to the constant bombardment of voices. Disturbing memories of people and places consumed my thoughts. Passively, I gave in to despair, stopped thinking and just let go. I had lost hope.

Even though people were all around me I ignored them. The staff urged me to sit up and socialize but I refused. Except for mealtimes I stayed on the couch. Days passed.

Every evening before bed I lined up with the others at the nurses' station to receive medication with a small plastic cup of juice. I was also given vitamins after tests revealed malnutrition. Andrea told me that the medication was an antipsychotic to make the voices go away. But it had little effect. They persisted and I still had trouble sleeping.

One afternoon I felt an inner restlessness. Finding it hard to be still I stopped lying on the couch and started pacing the hallways. When I found Andrea I complained to her.

"That could be akathisia," she said. "It's a side effect of the Stelazine you're taking. I'll talk to Dr. Taylor and we'll see what we can do."

Dr. Taylor was in charge of my treatment. I saw him, as well as a medical student, almost daily. Andrea and nursing assistants also asked about how I was getting along.

That evening when I received my medication I noticed two capsules in addition to the usual ones. I went to bed and within an hour fell asleep. About midnight I got up to go to the bathroom but half-way there I became faint and collapsed onto the floor. Through partially-opened eyes I vaguely saw two nurses bending over me, one holding my wrist while the other put a cuff around my arm.

"She's very pale," one said.

"It could be a reaction to the Mellaril," said the other.

I felt the cuff tighten.

"Her blood pressure is 58/40. That is dangerously low."

They discussed phoning the psychiatrist and helped me up. A nurse took my arm, assisting me to the bathroom and then back to my room. I slept fitfully through the rest of the night.

I did not receive medication the next day. The following evening I noticed pills of a color different from the ones I had been given before. With this change I experienced a day to day decrease in the volume and frequency of voices. After two weeks they had disappeared except for faint noises at bedtime and I started to sleep on a more consistent basis at night.

*

My reaction to the stillness was muted by the shock of what I had endured for almost two years. The onslaught from another realm had left me devastated. My newly found sanity was frail and my emotions, unsteady. I lacked perspective from which to reconcile the differing views of my predicament: the scientific materialism of modern psychiatry and what I had seen as a spiritual dimension. I had been labeled as having serious mental illness, schizophrenia, but I felt it was more than that. My only recourse was to follow the professionals responsible for my care and to trust in their wisdom.

During certain historical periods hearing voices, having visions and other extraordinary experiences were more accepted than today. In an article by Jerome Kroll and Bernard Bachrach titled *Visions and Psychopathology in the Middle Ages*, the authors state that during this period hallucinations were often attributed to religious experience instead of mental illness. Often, mystical states were thought to have a divine source and involve encounters with angelic beings. But some persons encountered demons thought to have a dark source. The experiences were only regarded as pathological when harmful to the individual or others.

In the scientific community spiritual or religious experiences are often discounted. Albert Schweitzer, in his book *THE PSYCHIATRIC STUDY OF JESUS: Exposition and Criticism*, gives an example of the divergence of psychiatric and religious views as exemplified in the opinions of philosopher and writer Emil Rasmussen. According to Schweitzer, Rasmussen sees Jesus and the prophets as madmen with diseased minds. Jesus, Rasmussen says, suffered from hallucinations as well as other symptoms that psychiatrists might label as psychosis.

Yet in another article, *Mystical Experience and Schizophrenia*, psychiatrist Peter Buckley expresses the view that mystical states and psychoses represent altered states of consciousness that have a common biology. He gives examples of psychotic episodes and mystical experiences and points out the similarities between them. Buckley concludes that the two have much in common, the primary difference being that psychotic episodes generate self-destructive acts, aggression and other negative consequences, whereas mystical experiences have a positive impact. Others have reached similar conclusions.

*

I took part in the daily routine of the ward. Over the course of several days Dr. Taylor allowed me to participate in more activities. On one occasion I joined some people learning how to do simple crafts like making pot holders. I went with a group to Donutland and down to an old basement room to listen to music. Eventually, he allowed me to go out on pass with my mother who took me to lunch. I did not receive therapy or counseling aimed at solving emotional problems. Drugs were the primary mode of treatment.

Even though I was more active I had not regained my concentration or ability to think in any kind of complex manner. I still found it difficult to read. Even television held my attention for only a few minutes at a time. I spent hours sitting in the dayroom staring at people. Still dwelling on the past I experienced the disturbing emotions that entailed: shame, for naively involving myself in a cult; rage, at those who had betrayed me; hopelessness, with no one to defend me.

After completing a month's stay on the ward, Melanie, the Women's Residence director, came and met with Dr. Taylor, Andrea, a social worker and me. By this time I was anxious to leave the hospital. We met around a table in the dayroom and Melanie encouraged me to move into the half-way house. She was a full-figured woman with a warm smile and her friendly demeanor helped put me at ease.

"We've just had an unexpected opening Marcia! You could move in as soon as you're discharged!"

I quickly responded, "Thank you—I'd like to."

I listened to Dr. Taylor explain my improvement to the others and then he looked at me and said, "You should continue to take the medication and see Dr. Hayes regularly. Do you hear voices any longer?"

Not sure of what to say I tried to answer as well as I could.

"No...no, not really. Not clear voices or words. Sometimes during the day I hear sounds like ocean waves breaking onto the shore. And at night before I fall to sleep there are soft noises by my ears. But that's all."

He seemed satisfied with my response and told Melanie that I could be released from his care. I was relieved that I would be leaving for the Residence. The next day my mother came and, together, we walked out of West Ward.

CHAPTER 11

The Women's Residence was located a few blocks from downtown. It was an older two-story house with a spacious interior that was once a private home. When the women and I were not busy with chores or talking with counselors we would gather in the livingroom, an area with drab gray and brown chairs, a couch, and cigarette smoke filling the air. Some had jobs; my roommate attended classes at the University. She was bright and studious but reticent, rarely interacting with anyone.

I met with a Vocational Rehabilitation counselor who enrolled me in that program. Its purpose was to evaluate my ability to work and to make recommendations about what I might be qualified to do. I would not be participating in this for several weeks and didn't know what to do in the meantime. One afternoon I painted watercolors at the diningroom table which gave me the opportunity to express feelings. Other days, I wandered around downtown. Television did not interest me. It was difficult to read. For the first time in years I had an opportunity to make friends and I struggled to do so.

One Sunday morning I walked to my childhood church which was only two blocks down the street. Sitting on an old wooden pew I worshipped the Christian God, the defender of the poor and oppressed. After the service drew to a close with prayer and singing the congregation filed out. I had met no one. I continued to attend when able but failed to gain any sense of belonging.

*

Five days after my release from the hospital I had an appointment with Dr. Hayes. At a counselor's suggestion I rode over on a University campus bus. When I walked into his office he seemed unchanged from the month before, reserved, yet kind. I started to convey to him the problems I had been having.

"I can't get interested in anything. I've tried to read but the books I find in the house are boring."

Dr. Hayes suggested I try the city library then asked how things were going for me at the residence. I described our various tasks then complained about my level of motivation, that I would lie in bed a lot and the counselors would get after me.

"I can't seem to cope."

"Do you still hear voices?" he asked.

"Since I left the hospital I hear faint sounds before I fall asleep at night in whichever ear touches my pillow."

Omitted from the discussion with Dr. Hayes was the heart of my problem. The turbulence and suffering caused by hallucinations combined with the cult experience had been debilitating. It had shaken the very foundation of my life. Rebuilding a fundamental stability was going to take time.

At some point I came to learn that hearing voices for an extended period was considered a psychotic episode. Hallucinations of this sort were the result of a chemical imbalance in the brain, a broken brain. The content of hallucinations was to be treated as chaotic nonsense, best ignored. Thus, the psychosis had no inherent meaning—or so they said....

*

Theorists in the field of transpersonal psychology have perspectives on psychosis that go beyond the chemical imbalance espoused by mainstream psychiatry. For example, psychiatrist John E. Nelson of *HEALING THE SPLIT: Integrating Spirit Into Our Understanding of the Mentally Ill,* explains that consciousness or mental awareness involves more than the workings of a physical brain. It also includes the state of the soul. This is in contrast to what many scientists believe. And while Nelson attributes madness to altered states of consciousness he concedes that it would be naïve to assume no connection between the immaterial mind and the brain for advances in neuroscience have clearly shown this to be the case. When delving into the nature of mental illness and manifestations such as hallucinations Nelson goes on to postulate that psychotic episodes can be a means of transformation. They can produce spiritual growth and maturity in those who experience them.

Stanislav Grof, also a psychiatrist, states in *HUMAN NATURE AND THE NATURE OF REALITY: Conceptual Challenges from Consciousness Research,* that "nonordinary" states of consciousness can lead to transformation of the mind and personality. What mainstream psychiatry and Western culture commonly label as psychosis may actually be what he has termed a "spiritual emergency." He and Nelson differentiate between "organic" or long-term schizophrenic illness and the shorter, temporary psychotic episodes that may not impair the individual in the long run. However, I disagree with this dichotomy and would place schizophrenia and the "spiritual emergency" on a continuum of pathological and paranormal experiences that have much in common.

In *MENTAL ILLNESS AND SPIRITUAL CRISIS: Implications for Psychiatric Rehabilitation,* psychologist Judith Miller uses the term "spiritual crisis" to define a psychotic episode that may involve struggle and conflict during a state of altered perception. The episode may be mystical in nature and, if thoughtfully considered and integrated into ordinary everyday consciousness, may have transformative potential. Such an encounter may import deep meaning to one who has experienced it.

*

I was again seated across the desk from Dr. Hayes, struggling to find words to express my feelings and thoughts.

"I still can't find any motivation to do the simplest things. The counselors get angry and I have to use every ounce of strength I have to do what is required. I'm bored and I can't enjoy anything. Life is too hard."

Dr. Hayes gave a few words of encouragement but they seemed to have no effect. Tears welled up in my eyes as I fumbled in my purse for a Kleenex.

"I don't have any energy. I feel hopeless about my future—I'm giving up!"

*

"Father wants us at Holy Rock—pronto!"

Just as we arrived at the top of the hill I saw Father brace himself with one hand and hoist himself on top of the boulder, Colonel Pak scrambling up beside him.

"Children, I have a message for you. Gather 'round quickly."

Someone beside me shoved for a better view; I took a step back.

"How do humans find happiness? What is our relationship to God?" Father called out passionately. "Every human is made up of essential duel components. In order for anything to maintain existence it needs energy and this applies to humans as well. Energy comes from give and take action and this requires a subject and object. Actions going in a straight line will eventually stop; therefore, eternal existence requires circular motion. When a subject and object have give and take, this allows circular motion. This is why I say that the eternal God has dual characteristics. And God made creation to be his eternal object so it, too, must have dual characteristics.

"We know God by looking at creation and in this way we can know God's character. God wanted to feel happiness so He created the universe. And man is at the center of the universe for the purpose of bringing joy to God. But in order for man to bring joy to God there has to be fulfillment of three great blessings. This can only be accomplished on the foundation of four positions and only then will a perfect object be established through which God can experience joy...."

Under the scorching heat of the afternoon sun I felt faint and longed to sit on the grass. Sweat trickled down my back. I shifted my weight from one foot to the other.

"God created humankind to rule the universe. God does not rule the universe directly but He has given dominion of the world to man. He has chosen me to instruct man on how to rule the universe. God gave me The Divine Principle to unite humankind to Himself. Live this principle—act upon it. Then Satan cannot invade. When you are completely united with The Divine Principle Satan cannot take you away from God. When you live this truth, as I am, you will bring joy to God which is our purpose. Live as I live—I am The Divine Principle—it is in me. I embody the truth...."

While in the cult I had lost my self. Not only was my personality destroyed, gone was a sense of who or what I was as a human being. Medication was supposed to fill this void and give me back a sound mind and a core of strength from which to go forward; however, I felt like I had been in a battle and the enemy had won.

But...the war wasn't over yet.

*

After forty minutes the session started to wind down. My eyes turned to the foxtail fern on the corner of Dr. Hayes' desk. It was the same one that I had seen there over a year ago.

"I really like your plant. It looks so healthy and strong."

After a brief pause Dr. Hayes said, "You can have it if you'd like."

"Thank you," I said, reaching over and picking up the plant.

Then with a worried expression Dr. Hayes filled out a prescription, stood, and handed it to me.

"This is antidepressant medication. Take one tablet at bedtime for several days then increase the dose to two a day. Why don't you come back in a week."

I put the prescription in my purse and with my plant walked out the door.

An ally.

*

The Voc Rehab evaluation program was held at a University compound on the outskirts of town. I went through a series of tasks consisting of menial labor. The counselors observed me as I worked, measuring my ability to get things done efficiently and in a timely manner. I followed instructions and found that no special skills were required. It was also repetitious. But I remembered my father saying when I was young, "All work has dignity," so I did the best I could.

During the four weeks I participated in the evaluation the emptiness and despair inside me became so great that at one point I could no longer function. I sat down in a chair and simply said that I couldn't go on. The counselors had me withdraw. My hope that the program could help me was, therefore, short-lived.

One day in May I went to another appointment with Dr. Hayes. They were now bi-monthly. He began.

"How are you feeling today?"

I pushed my hair back from my face and, as I often did, looked out the window behind Dr. Hayes. Spring rains made the grass a vivid green.

"I'm unhappy but I don't know whether it is something in me or caused by my environment or surroundings. The women in the residence are very sick and the place is not well kept. The atmosphere is not uplifting; it's dreary."

Dr. Hayes did not comment but asked, "Are you having hallucinations?"

"I hear a kind of rushing sound like a strong wind blowing or a waterfall, but it doesn't speak to me. It wasn't there earlier. I would like to be rid of any reminder that I am schizophrenic. That label is an insult."

We discussed my withdrawal from the evaluation program and how I had felt there. Toward the end of the session an idea came to me that had occurred earlier in the week.

"I've always found it easier to talk to a woman so, besides these sessions, I'd like to have a woman counselor. During my high school years I saw a nurse at the Mental Health

Center but I haven't talked to her since I returned to Iowa City. Do you think you could set up an appointment for me?"

While jotting down a note Dr. Hayes answered, "I can arrange for you to be seen there. Meanwhile, I suggest that you increase your antidepressant to three tablets and the antipsychotic to three also. These medications work slowly but are apt to improve the way you are feeling. I'll see you in two weeks."

CHAPTER 12

"Just be happy!"

According to Renee, the newly hired counselor, this was the solution to all our problems. Showering her beauty queen smile upon us the women sat patiently in the livingroom waiting for dinner. I wondered where she had gotten her training.

"It's not that easy," I said feeling my face grow warm.

"You seem so angry Marcia!" Renee responded, folding her arms across her chest.

"No one understands," I said. "I've tried to do everything I've been told. Over the past several months I've attempted to work. First, I folded clothes at a laundry in one hundred degree heat with an emotionally unstable boss standing over me. And when that didn't work out I tried waitressing. But that terrified me. It is against my nature to interact with the public so closely. I was supposed to write down orders and serve food as fast as possible, then clear off dishes from the tables—the pressure was just too great! And customers yelled at me when I didn't do things fast enough! I just couldn't take it!"

"Dinner's ready," someone announced dispassionately from the kitchen doorway. And with that the discussion ended. During the meal there was little conversation and, afterwards, most of the women watched TV. Before going to bed that evening I watered the fern I had placed on a platform near the bottom of the stairway. Some of its leaves were turning yellow and brown.

In the morning I struggled to get out of bed. The medication I had been taking caused drowsiness so I needed several cups of coffee in order to function. I made it to the kitchen, had breakfast, and after a shower was ready for my appointment with the psychiatric nurse at the Mental Health Center.

I was sitting in the reception area of the center when the nurse called my name then showed me to her office.

"Take any chair," she said and smiled, motioning with her hand.

I chose a rocking chair with a red cushion and she took another immobile one opposite me. Except for a few streaks of gray in her brown hair and some lines on her face she looked like I remembered her. Glancing around, I saw bay windows with sunlight streaming through onto a half-dozen plants.

"How have you been Marcia? It's been many years since I've seen you."

Feeling embarrassed, I had trouble getting words out.

"I've had some problems....I haven't been feeling well."

But she jumped right in.

"Would you like to talk about that? What has been troubling you? You're a young woman now—does it have to do with sexuality? Is that what's been troubling you? Why don't we talk about sex!"

She gazed at me nonchalantly as if she had just asked if I'd like a cup of tea. But startled by her suggestion I just looked away and mumbled, "I'd rather not."

She went on, "I specialize in sex therapy. So if you have any questions about this topic feel free to bring them up. Now, what would you rather talk about?"

After thirty minutes discussing my experiences over the past several years, I left feeling drained and weak. The session had not been helpful. I decided not to go back.

As the days passed I felt increasingly useless and unwanted. Seeking male companionship I went to a disco a few times with several of the residents. A few men asked me to dance but I found them unattractive. I spent most of the time watching people while sipping drinks. I thought it was not a good place to meet desirable men and gave up the search.

Still interested in religion I decided to attend a Bible study group that was held at a Baptist student center near the half-way house. I enjoyed reading scripture but also sought new friends. I didn't know what to say in conversations, though, and this put me at a disadvantage. They shied away from me and I didn't know the reason. I was perplexed as to why I couldn't make friends. I finally stopped going.

*

October arrived and Melanie informed me it was time I moved out of the residence. She said the program had done all it could for me and other women were waiting to get in. Over the next several weeks my mother and I searched for an apartment and found one near the City Park along the Iowa River. The complex had originally been University student housing but was now converted to public use. It still resembled a dormitory with a reception desk where the manager kept watch over the comings and goings of renters. On the first floor was a lounge with a TV, study area with shelves of magazines, a swimming pool, and a billiard room.

I was able to pay rent because I received government benefits for the disabled. One was called Supplementary Security Income (SSI) and the other was Section Eight or public housing assistance. Along with these I used Food Stamps for groceries and Medicaid took care of my medical and dental expenses.

Within a few days of signing the lease my mother helped me move in. I decorated the walls with pictures donated by some of my relatives and I bought a large world map for the area over my desk. I lacked motivation for many things but managed to keep the apartment clean.

The church I had been attending was now farther away. I went less often and then, because I had to walk, quit altogether when cold winter weather set in. I started to drift away from religion. I joined an organization called Young Singles of America. Meetings were only once a month and the people were hard to relate to. Many seemed lifeless and, eventually, one man killed himself.

*

Stigmatization is the term used to describe treatment that when occurring makes people feel that others are looking down on them and considering them inferior, defective or abnormal. A source of society's prejudice has been misinformation about mental illness and this has made it difficult for me to make friends. In the past, when people learned I had schizophrenia, they assumed I had split or multiple personalities which is not the case. I've had to explain to people that psychiatrists call that illness multiple personality or dissociative disorder, the official term in the *DIAGNOSTIC AND STATISTICAL MANUAL OF MENTAL DISORDERS [DSM-IV]*. I've told them that schizophrenia involves symptoms such as: hallucinations (auditory and/or visual), delusions, thought disorder, apathy, and withdrawal. It affects one percent of the population and is among the ten leading causes of disability among young adults. It usually begins in the teens or early twenties and, for most, makes normal life—school, work, family—impossible.

The public is not aware that people with mental illness are more likely to be victims of violence than perpetrators of it. In the course of my own life I have spent more time in fear of other people's aggression than in committing my own. The media often sensationalizes the random violent acts of a few people with mental illness, thereby promoting stereotypes and fears.

*

I was still hungry for companionship. Evenings, I would phone one of my parents and talk a few minutes, but as time went on it became burdensome for them. My mother graciously drove me to the grocery store every week and sometimes to lunch. Often, to be near people, I would take the bus downtown or ride around the city on its route. Occasionally, I would drop in at the half-way house during visitor's hours in search of someone to talk with. Once, my old roommate and I went out for coffee.

These contacts lasted a few hours leaving the rest of my day empty. I felt isolated and spent hours looking out my window watching traffic go by. As months went on I found fewer people available. The hours at the window grew longer and one afternoon I began to think about taking an overdose of aspirin as I had when I was a teen. Finally, when I could stand it no longer I went to the phone and called Dr. Hayes. His secretary put me through.

"Hello, Marcia."

"I'm thinking of taking an overdose—I feel horrible. What should I do?"

"Would you like to come in tomorrow to go over things? Around eleven would be a good time."

I felt I could hold out until then.

"I'll be there."

The following day I rose earlier than usual and as was my habit meticulously groomed myself. I took the bus over to the hospital and went to Dr. Hayes' office where, once again, I found him behind his desk. He put down a journal he had been reading and stood to greet me, then we both sat down.

"How are you doing today? Is there any change from yesterday?"

I remained silent.

"When you are depressed what do you think about?"

"I don't have enough friends. I don't see my mother as much as I'd like. I don't think I'll ever be able to get married or have children. The men who have been interested in me are not my type."

Dr. Hayes did not comment so I added, "I don't feel able to work and I can't do other things I would like to do….I feel bored all the time."

"Are you able to get up in the morning?"

"I usually go to bed at nine and get up at noon. I am groggy in the morning from the medication. Once I'm up I can only motivate myself to do essential things. Other than that I am at loose ends. Someone said I'm vegetating. That makes me angry—people don't understand!"

Quite often relatives and counselors voiced disapproval of my lack of ambition or motivation, the failure to keep jobs or to be productive. This apathy on my part was something I could not control in spite of my willful search and struggle to rise above it. Sometimes this problem was a side-effect of medication. At other times depression and feelings of weakness to the point of immobility were so over-powering I could not function. So I was accused of being lazy because I appeared to be wallowing in self-pity and hopelessness—as though by choice.

In their book *MODELS OF MADNESS, MODELS OF MEDICINE,* Miriam Siegler and Humphry Osmond delineate the major models of mental illness. They say that according to the moral model the mentally ill person's behavior is judged "bad" or immoral and in need of correction. Relatives of the sick person try to discipline him or her into acting appropriately. By contrast, the medical model places the ill person in the "sick" role and suspends moral judgment in the hope of finding a pharmacological means of modification. This model places the blame for the illness on the genetic, chemical, or other physical abnormalities, not on the patient.

"I'd hate to see you give up on yourself," Dr. Hayes said.

"I'm depressed when I'm alone. I'm unstable...."

"Do you want to come into the hospital?"

"I'd rather not."

I didn't like the idea of being locked up.

"Any time you feel the inclination to harm yourself you can come into the hospital simply by letting me know. I doubt that an increase in the antidepressant medication will alter your mood but there is no reason not to give this a try. If you continue to feel depressed as you have been I think we should have you come in. Through a change in medication or some modification in plans we can try to alter the situation."

"Okay," I said, "I'll keep that in mind and stay in touch with you."

After Dr. Hayes specified the amount of increase in the antidepressant I thanked him and left. While at my appointment a winter storm had brought sub-zero temperatures and blizzard-like conditions. Making my way home I hoped that somehow in the future things would be different.

*

January 1979 arrived and my situation was much the same. The holidays had been a trial; I felt like a stranger amongst my relatives. I could not afford to buy presents which brought further distance. Now, a week after New Year's, I was alone at night. I had just finished washing the dishes and had placed two bright red apples in a fruit bowl decorating my kitchen table. Dinner had been my mother's homemade spaghetti and a lettuce salad. I would not be seeing her for several days at which point we would be going to the grocery store. Sitting down, bent over the table, I put my head in my hands and began to think. Television didn't interest me and it was another night alone. I didn't know what to do. I felt I needed contact with another human being. Tears fell as I remembered Dr. Hayes' words: "If you continue to feel depressed we should have you come into the hospital."

I got up from the table and phoned my mother.

"Mom, would you take me to the hospital?"

Apparently surprised she said, "Why? What's wrong?"

"I'm thinking of overdosing on my meds. I feel so lonely."

"Don't do that!" she said. "I'll be right over. Pack some clothes in a bag."

"Okay."

At the hospital I was interviewed once again by a young psychiatric resident though this one's face looked worn and exhausted with dark circles under his eyes. Out of his white coat pocket a stethoscope dangled precariously.

He was blunt.

"Why are you here?"

"I'm tired," I said, "really tired of not being able to function."

"What do you do during the day to pass the time?"

"Sometimes I ride the bus or window shop. If there is a friend here in the hospital I'll visit her. I usually don't read or watch TV; I sit around crying—I cry a lot. I never have any energy."

The resident continued with questions. I told him of my most recent attempt at volunteering at a preschool. I quit because of low mood, boredom, and lack of motivation.

"How would you state your main problem?" he asked.

I paused a moment and then said, "It's a lack of interest and pleasure in life. I have been doing practically nothing and this bothers me although I have no better idea of how to improve my situation. And I'm usually so lonely I just want to kill myself."

This time I was admitted to East Ward where I shared a room with three other women. The routine of meals and dispensation of medication was the same as it had been on West Ward. During the first week of my stay my mood improved. I enjoyed being around the people.

Ever since my involvement in the cult my emotional maturity had lagged behind that of my peers. Even though I was twenty-four years old chronologically, I was much younger emotionally. For most adults being in a mental hospital would be unpleasant, yet at this time in my life it was better than living in my apartment. I enjoyed the presence of the other patients and caring staff. In later years I discovered a letter written during this stay. It revealed the change of mood brought on by hospitalization.

Dear Grandma,

Hi! Right now I'm in psych hospital. They have good meals here and fun activities. Last night I played volleyball. This morning I played billiards. Mom and I just got back from going on a walk. Tonight we're going to a movie.

My girlfriend, Cheryl is in psych also. She's a lot sicker than I am. She needs a lot more attention. Last night she didn't sleep at all.

Tomorrow, the hospital is having music activity, ice cream at Baskin Robins, crafts, and a dance at night. Friday, there is bowling and miniature golf.

I'm thinking of working at Goodwill through Vocational Rehabilitation. I quit that a while back but think I'll try it again.

I've had trouble waking up in the mornings at home but in the hospital I've gotten up and dressed without much trouble. I came into the hospital because I had suicidal thoughts. I got discouraged....

*

During the third week of my stay I was given individual outing privileges and I would leave for hours at a time. On one occasion I went to a bank where I bought a bus pass, to a hair salon to make an appointment, and I purchased greeting cards at a store where I also bought a cup of coffee. Then when I came back to the hospital I was led by a nurse to the second floor for psychological testing involving some multiple choice questions and other things.

Four weeks passed and the physician in charge of my care met with me. As we sat in the dayroom I was distracted by the dozen or so patients and staff around us. I had to make an extra effort to hear what the doctor was saying.

"Marcia, I'm thinking of discharging you in a few days. I doubt that you had a depressive illness that would have responded to antidepressant medication, so I took you off Norpramine. We've helped you re-establish a normal sleep pattern. Maybe when you are released Dr. Hayes can help you find ways to motivate yourself to do volunteer work again or some other productive activity. Do you have any questions?"

I couldn't think of anything to say.

"No."

The doctor stood and, taking the keys from his pocket, walked quickly towards the locked doors. As he left I had mixed emotions. Leaving the hospital meant freedom but I was troubled at the thought of returning to the isolation of my apartment.

Three days later I was back home staring out the window watching the traffic go by.

*

Philip Yancey, in *THE JESUS I NEVER KNEW*, quotes Mother Teresa who at one time ran a clinic for lepers in Calcutta. She said that she has medication for people with diseases like leprosy but that drugs don't treat the most significant problem which is "the disease of being *unwanted*." She said sick people who live in poverty suffer more from being an outcast than from material deprivation. The worst poverty is feeling lonely and unwanted.

Those with mental illness are the lepers of Western culture.

*

With Dr. Hayes' encouragement I went back to Vocational Rehabilitation. In March they enrolled me in the Goodwill plant where I worked as a store clerk. I straightened shelves that had vases, books, and other items. I also sorted racks of outdated clothes. It was part-time, paying less than two dollars an hour. As at the evaluation program, I again felt empty and depressed so I quit after two weeks. The low pay gave little incentive and the tasks were too simple. My co-workers were distant and unfriendly. Still, giving up on this felt like another failure.

Having drifted away from my spiritual beliefs I also lacked the hope faith could bring. One day at an appointment with Dr. Hayes he brought up the topic of spirituality. He spoke in a slow, deliberate, and precise manner, seeming to choose his words carefully.

"Do you…believe in God?"

I glanced away and thought a moment then looked at him directly.

"I want to…" I said softly, "but I can't."

I began to focus on that which I felt was within my own control. Forgetting about the spiritual aspect of existence and higher aspirations for employment, I turned my attention to my social life. Wanting to break free from isolation I felt I must find a male companion, an intellectual equal and lover. I thought if I lost weight this might improve my chances of finding a husband. As a result I became obsessed with food, calories, exercise and the scale. At the end of five months I had lost twenty pounds.

It was now August and I was slowly regaining my mental abilities. During the past year I had been unable to motivate myself to read a book. But I now ventured into the study area of the complex and found on the magazine rack *TIME, NEWSWEEK, and U.S. NEWS AND WORLD REPORT.* I read them with interest and felt better because of it. This got me started on reading other things.

I also began watching the TV in the lounge hoping to meet some of the other tenants. One evening, a local newscast had a segment on the International Writers' Program held every fall at the University. A reporter interviewed an attractive young author with wire-rim glasses and curly dark hair. Just after the program ended that same man who was interviewed walked into the lounge.

"I just saw you on TV!" I said.

"It was filmed earlier today," he said and smiled.

We talked, began dating, and became friends.

After a few months the writer returned to his own country. I then felt motivated to get a job and worked in a big department store's office to save for air fare for visiting my friend. We wrote letters.

I took a bus across town and once at the office concentrated on clerical tasks under constant pressure from my supervisor. But often as I worked in my own room I would be forced to put my hands on my desk and rest my head during attacks from hallucinations—not clear voices, but babbling noises. I thought I had telepathic powers and could sense my boss trying to control my mind. Often, I heard evil spirit music, a remnant of sounds I had heard while in the cult.

Not being able to finish the assigned work on some days, I was reprimanded. The stress caused by interacting with co-workers was unnerving. One young woman, a high-school drop-out, enjoyed taunting me as I passed by her desk to into my room. After lunch she would sneer, "There's Marcia, scurrying back to her hole! There she goes!"

For months, I saved almost every penny I earned. I thought things were going well when, one day, I received a phone call. A man from the Social Security office said that I had been over-paid in benefits since I had income from my job. He tried to explain the system to me but I didn't understand what was going on and felt very confused. I found out that I had to give the government all my savings and that left nothing for my trip. I was so depressed I quit the job. My friend and I started to drift apart. Eventually, we quit writing.

I was back where I started.

CHAPTER 13

I had now entered a spiritual wasteland. There I wandered for many years lost, seeking guidance from evening stars to lead me out of the desert. The journey began with Vinay.

*

"I didn't know you smoked," a young East Indian said as he lit up a Camel and took a drag.

"Yes, I do," I said, exhaling a cloud. We stood at the entrance of the TV lounge. I had come down from my apartment after dinner to watch the evening news. He and I had not formally met but from his remark it was evident that I had caught his attention.

"Would you like to go out for a drink?" he asked and then smiled at which point I noticed a crooked front tooth that in no way detracted from his charm.

"My name's Vinay Shah, *Dr.* Shah. I'm a post doc in chemistry. I do research."

He seems proud of himself, I thought, *and perhaps rightly so.*

We went out for a drink.

Outside of his working hours Vinay became my constant companion. We frequented bars where he always got drunk. If we did not go out he would drink heavily at his or my apartment. I soon learned that besides being an alcoholic, he was a playboy. He flirted with co-eds at every chance. Once he even left me in the movie theater at the Union to hit on a young woman one floor below in the student lounge.

When his behavior alienated me he would fix us a curry-dish meal or show me how he did his work in the lab. These things always impressed me and I would reinstate him.

Several weeks after becoming involved with Vinay I had my monthly appointment with Dr. Hayes. It was summertime and the office was cool from air conditioning. I sat down and took off my sunglasses, replacing them with clear ones. I had looked forward to sharing the news that I had a new man in my life. We spoke for a few minutes about my medication and then I decided to tell him.

"I've been seeing someone. He's from India and is a post doc in chemistry."

Dr. Hayes glanced down at his desk then looked up at me and said, "You mean a graduate student."

"No, a post doc. He has his Ph.D already," I said emphatically, my voice clearly showing annoyance.

He had not asked a question. He had attempted—or so it appeared—to correct me. At first, I was offended. Then I became enraged. He was implying I wasn't good enough to date a man with a Ph.D. Who, after all, would want a schizophrenic? I glared at him.

My mind felt part of an emotional paradox: I was full of pride that I was so intelligent as to land a scientist and the prestige it brought; and yet, as a mental patient, a schizophrenic, no less, I felt I belonged at the bottom of society. Dr. Hayes, for whatever reason, ignited a furious reaction in me that prompted a rash decision. I saw this as an unpardonable insult and decided to leave with no intention of returning.

"I have to go," I said, grabbing my purse and getting up. "I'm leaving."

Walking out, I silently vowed to never speak to him again. But in doing so I abandoned the only sympathizer to my cause, the only person who had had the patience to listen to the struggles I had so far endured. And now he would not be there to coach me on those that were to come. As I terminated therapy I stopped taking medications as well.

I was on my own.

*

Vinay convinced me to move into his apartment located in a suburb of Iowa City. This meant I had to give up my governmental housing assistance, a benefit not easy to come by. But being dependent on Vinay for shelter soon proved to be a trap. He was sadistic and most evenings would drink heavily and call me names. Each night he became more hostile. He became the embodiment of demons. The psychotic voices of my past now spoke through him.

"Leave me alone!" I screamed at him. Then in the morning he would be sweet and kind, convincing me not to leave him. This pattern continued and I could not break free from the relationship.

In the midst of this turmoil I enrolled in the community college's secretarial program. Vocational Rehabilitation funded my studies. They had tested and found me qualified for the University but that seemed intimidating and I opted for something less demanding.

From the first day of class the other students knew I was different because my funding from Voc Rehab was loudly announced by the teacher when she specified the payment that was due. From that moment no one treated me as an equal. They made me feel that as a disabled person I was not worthy of their friendship. No one spoke to me unless it was necessary and on those occasions they were curt. So for the next nine months I rarely conversed with classmates. But I enjoyed the work and lived only to please my instructors. At grading time I received High Honors.

By this time I had quit smoking and ceased drinking with Vinay though I was still living with him. One night I went to bed early, leaving him to watch television by himself. After a while I drifted off but soon felt warmth, as if a fire, near my face. I opened my eyes and was startled to see Vinay holding a glowing cigarette near my cheek. Horrified, I backed away just in time. He was amused.

"Wouldn't that look great, Marcia?!" he said and laughed. "You could live the rest of your life with a burn scar on your face! Wouldn't that look pretty?!"

I sprang out of bed and called a taxi. My mother let me stay with her a couple of nights while I searched for a room to rent. I found one in an old house in a densely populated student district. Vinay continued to harass me with phone calls and by banging on my door. He obtained his Green Card and made plans to work for Monsanto. Though he pursued me he was also aware that his parents intended to arrange a marriage for him. Springtime came and he left for India, returning a married man. Still, he pursued me and I felt my only recourse was to make myself unattractive to him. I remembered Vinay saying, "I will never date a woman with short hair."

So I cut my hair.

Standing in front of a bathroom mirror I took a scissors and snipped away my long locks, disregarding the uneven neckline. It worked. Soon after, he left me alone and was out of my life. Then I bought a blue parakeet to keep me company that I named Baby.

Because of this turmoil it was harder to concentrate in school. I was lonely, isolated, and depressed. The whole stormy year, now in its conclusion, had robbed me of my stamina. So I withdrew from the bookkeeping course and this meant an Incomplete for the program. Mourning my loss at the end of the semester, I drew thick lines around the bottom of my eyes with black makeup, an exaggeration of the fashion. I took on the part of the class crazy person and left in disgrace.

*

Summer of 1981 arrived and the daytime temperature outside was over one hundred degrees. I lived in a room on the second floor of an old house with no air conditioning. Night had fallen and I got out of bed to run cold water over wash cloths to place on my forehead. The fan blew warm air and offered little benefit. Back in bed I tossed and turned until two a.m., then gave up and turned on my black and white TV. I watched until dawn.

As I boiled water on my single hot plate for coffee I noticed a strange silence. I turned to the bird cage and was startled to see my parakeet lying on the bottom. *Baby has died!* Tears filled my eyes, I felt a mounting pressure in my chest and I wept. My little friend was gone. I wrapped Baby in a towel and buried him in the back yard.

That afternoon in the sweltering heat I realized that I could go to my mother's apartment and enjoy air conditioning. With this in mind I gathered a few belongings and started out on a four-mile walk. Halfway there I began to feel faint. My eyes were drawn to the cars going by, their windows closed and passengers in cool comfort. I thought they were mocking me. I saw jeers on their faces and thought they were speaking telepathically.

"Dumb woman, walking down the street! Why don't you have a car like everybody else?! Go ahead, suffer in the hot sun! See if we care!"

I thought they hated me and were laughing. I concentrated on putting one foot ahead of the other. The sun's rays seemed to pass through my clothes, burning my skin. Finally, I reached my mother's apartment, took the key from my purse, and went in. When my mother came home from work she was surprised but welcomed me. I stayed several days then went back to the oppressive heat.

Two other women rented on my floor. We shared a refrigerator which led one to believe we also shared food which was not the original plan. As a result I kept as many groceries as possible in my room but then found I was sharing them with the mice. Insects were also abundant which were particularly fond of my bed.

I spend the next year working at various jobs, one being a clerk-typist in Medical Records at the University Hospital. The work was so consuming that after working hours I was incapable of social interaction. Next, I was hired to work mornings as a mother's helper.

I continued to be frustrated with my social life, dating men who I learned to be dishonest and finding the women I knew, uncaring. One of them, however, took me to a drop-in program at the Mental Health Center. This was a place where psychiatric patients could meet to have coffee, play board games, and socialize. My return to the psychiatric system began here. About that time I was hired at Sears and also began treatment with a psychiatrist at the center. At our first meeting he prescribed a small dose of antipsychotic medication. He eventually added Valium, a medication used to treat anxiety.

Interactions with my relatives had been sparse though I went to holiday gatherings and occasional family dinners. On one occasion my father spoke of a half-way house for people who had been in cults and then deprogrammed. Its purpose, he said, was to help people adjust to regular society again. It was located near Cedar Hill Park. He suggested that I contact this program and find someone to talk to about my experiences. So one winter day I went to this place. It sat on a hill with a long driveway leading up to it. I knocked and the door was opened by a woman with a solemn expression.

"Yes, may I help you?"

"Hello," I said. "I was told that this is a half-way house for people who've been in cults, then deprogrammed. Do I have the right address?"

Suddenly, she became alive; her face lit up with a radiating smile.

"Yes! Yes! You have the right place! Come right in, come in!" she said.

And I did.

A younger woman sat in a livingroom chair with a book in her lap. As I entered, her eyes became round and seemingly fixed on the ongoing scene.

"I'm Misty," said the woman who had opened the door. "What brings you here? What's your name?"

Ignoring her request for my identity I said, "I was in the Unification Church a while back and went through deprogramming. I came to see what you do here."

"Well, you've come to the right place. Let me show you around. Come this way—

Suddenly, the door opened again and a man with a suitcase burst into the room.

"Hi, Misty! I just got in from Dallas! The trip went well!"

"Hi, Brandon! Welcome back!" Misty said.

"How did everything go?" the other woman said.

"Really well," he said. "It's great to be back but the weather here is a shock! I left eighty degree temps!"

Then looking toward me he asked, "What do we have here?"

Still refusing to give my name I looked at Misty, "Did you say you'd give a tour?"

"Sure….Brandon, this woman stopped by to learn about our program. I'm going to show her around," she said and proceeded to guide me through the various rooms of the house.

The first stop was the kitchen. On each cupboard was a label describing the contents within. Even the canisters and drawers were labeled neatly which I thought odd.

Most bedrooms had bunkbeds in groups of twos, the larger ones had more. Everything was in perfect order giving the impression of military style. No decorations and little color. It reminded me of the cult. As Misty and I rejoined Brandon and the other woman I noticed they even dressed like people in the cult. Also, Moon was always flying people around the country; this was one of the methods he used to impress members.

From the time I was told of this "half-way" house I had suspected trouble. I had prepared myself for deception and now felt my suspicions seemed warranted. The regimented atmosphere, the austerity and bunk beds supported my idea that this was a place used to coax vulnerable deprogrammed ex-cult members to rejoin. In their fragile emotional states they would be susceptible.

Misty asked me to take a seat but I remained standing. She picked up a pen and writing pad and turning toward me said, "How long has it been since you left the Unification Church? I can provide counseling sessions for you but it would be more helpful if you moved in. Where are you living now?"

Trusting my instincts I backed off and moved toward the door.

"Not so fast! I don't believe you are who you say you are! This is exactly the kind of thing Moon would do to try to draw former members back in! I think this house has been set up for deceiving old cult members and I'm not going to fall for it! Sorry!"

I swiftly opened the door and walked outside leaving Misty and the others apparently struggling with what to say. They remained silent. As I headed toward home I felt my face warm from anger, soothed by the frigid wind.

*

In 1982 Moon was put on trial for tax evasion. He lost the case but appealed to the Supreme Court before being sent to federal prison for eighteen months. Moon, a con-artist, fabricated a religious story with which to manipulate his followers. His organization uses brain-washing techniques similar to those used against American soldiers during the Korean War such as sleep and nutritional deprivation, mental programming, and emotional abuse. Moon and his leaders have created a totalitarian regime that has fundraising as its primary aim. While he and his leaders have lived in luxury his supporters live in poverty and his organization has established over a hundred corporations around the world as fronts for the cult.

Though Moon spent time in jail more should be done to prevent his followers from recruiting members in the United States under the guise of evangelism, for his conviction did not stop his organization from operating here.

Moon left the United States and I don't know if he is still alive. He expanded his activities to countries in South America such as Brazil and Paraguay where he bought large tracts of land.

*

In fall of 1983 I enrolled in a philosophy course at the University. Again, I found joy in learning; however, my personal life was in such chaos that I struggled to finish the work. Toward finals time I became so distraught that I had to ask the instructor for an extension and he allowed me to take the test a week later. I then gave up the idea of more schooling.

One day in mid-winter a Sunday school teacher from the Lutheran church I had stopped attending phoned and asked that I speak to her high school class about my experience in the cult. On the morning of my talk there was a snow storm so I took a taxi which was a big expense for me.

I gave the young people a vivid description of my recruitment, indoctrination, and brainwashing, and of my departure from the cult. I explained that while in the cult I had become psychotic and was now being treated for mental illness. The group expressed interest and asked some questions. When I left I hoped my visit would keep them from falling prey as I had to one of the many groups targeting America's youth.

Soon after, I contacted Dr. Hayes to ask if I might be reinstated as his patient. It had been three years since I had seen him. One afternoon, with the hope he would respond favorably, I wrote the following letter:

> Dear Dr. Hayes,
>
> For the past couple of years I have seen a psychiatrist at the Mental Health Center. Since he recently retired I am wondering if you would be able to prescribe medications for me. I work part-time at Sears: three-hour shifts, four days a week in the Receiving Department and occasionally, Fashions.
>
> To help you understand my current state I'll give the following description: I experience a lot of anxiety and I think it comes from how extremely sensitive I am to other people's remarks and opinions. I do not sleep well and my sleep pattern is erratic. Often, I go to bed early and awaken at 4:00 in the morning. I get a lot of headaches, wear out easily, and am often

fatigued. I am very sensitive to everyday stress and I get nervous a lot.

When I'm stressed more than usual I sometimes hallucinate or have telepathic powers. Also, I sometimes believe that men are controlling my thoughts or putting thoughts into my head.

Sometimes, I am overwhelmed by waves of anger which bring me to the point of violence although I am never that way. At other times I am depressed and have thoughts of hopelessness and committing suicide. I don't have much motivation for things I need or like to do.

Do you think some medication might help with the anxiety? A psychiatrist prescribed Valium once but it didn't help; it mostly made me drowsy. He also gave me Loxitane but I couldn't tell if that helped either. And I don't remember if the Navane you prescribed several years ago made any difference.

If I can start seeing you again, would you set up the first appointment?

Thank you very much….

CHAPTER 14

"Hi, I'm Don. I was studying to be a Jesuit priest when I got schizophrenia."

Before me stood a large bespectacled man with several days' growth of beard on his face.

"I'm forty-two now; that happened back in the sixties. I managed to go back to school, though, to get a degree in sociology at the University. It took me ten years to finish, but I did it."

Don and I stood by a kitchen sink, a reminder of the drop-in center's former use as an apartment. On his Iowa sweatshirt covering his vast belly were stains of ketchup and chocolate drippings.

"I used to be a tennis instructor before I got sick," I said. "When I graduated from high school I was asked to workout with tennis pros in California, but decided to teach in a nearby town instead."

Don's eyes opened wide and he gasped for breath.

"Wow! My sister, Mandy, was a tennis pro years ago and even played at Wimbledon! Now, she's a mother and works in real estate in the northwest."

What I had told Don about my athletic background was true and I was soon to learn that what he had said to me about his sister was true as well.

Just then Ellen, who was the coordinator, called out to us asking if we would like to sit with the small group who were on chairs lining the walls.

"Don, Marcia, come join us."

Peering through clouds of smoke I found a seat, but Don left. I heard his heavy footsteps as he went down the stairs. I wanted to know more about these people so I asked them about themselves. Some eagerly responded.

"I wanted to be an elementary school teacher," said a slender, shaggy-haired man. After snuffing out a cigarette he lit up another. He smiled and then addressed the group.

"If number two pencils are the most popular, why are they still called number two?!"

The room erupted in laughter which sliced through the dejected atmosphere. Smiles appeared where before there had only been sad expressions. We had come here seeking sustenance, food for our souls. Sometimes, this came in the form of laughter.

I had been an outcast in secretarial school and on the job after I revealed details of my background. People turned away. They stopped talking to me. Since this center opened, I, along with many others had found camaraderie here. Spending time together we formed a community, a subculture, to lick our wounds and gather strength before going back out into the world. Relationships formed helped us to maintain some stability and were a welcome diversion from the psychiatric ward.

"I've tried to kill myself at least a dozen times in the past eight years—I get so angry!" said a petite blond woman.

"Is that why you do it? Because you're angry?" I asked. I noticed numerous scars on her forearms.

"I can't explain it, really. I don't know why I do it."

Members called her Cedra. I wanted to initiate a friendship but she seemed too aloof and self-absorbed. I thought I'd wait until a better time.

Ellen, a tall, beautiful brunette, had a natural mother earth quality about her. As she joined in the conversation I found myself impressed by her mind. She did not have a college degree but her common sense and wisdom made up for it. She was articulate, compassionate, and eager to help. I sensed she was someone I could open up to.

"Could I meet with you on a regular basis to talk?" I asked.

"Sure," she said, "I'll get my calendar; let's set up an appointment."

I started meeting with Ellen once a week. Also, the drop-in center was open three hours in the afternoons except on weekends and I attended when I wasn't working. I learned that those of us who gathered here were poor—poor in spirit as well as financial resources. This contributed to our bond. We, the rejected ones, found at the center a sympathetic ear and kind word. For many of us there was little else we looked forward to.

*

In July 1984 I resumed monthly appointments with Dr. Hayes. It had been three years since I walked out on him. On the first day back near two o'clock one afternoon, I sat in the reception area of a new psychiatric clinic awaiting his entrance. It had been relocated to the second floor of another wing of the hospital. The modern blue and gray furnishings were accented with pastel acrylic paintings on the walls. Adjacent to these, mini-blinds covered broad windows. A dozen other patients of all ages sat quietly, waiting for their therapists.

"Marcia."

Looking up from my *NEWSWEEK* I saw Dr. Hayes and set the magazine down. I walked over and he reached out to shake in greeting.

Taking his hand, I said, "Hello, Dr. Hayes."

We walked along a hallway to his office in silence. We sat down.

"How have you been?" he asked.

Dr. Hayes seemed thinner than I remembered him being but had the same solemn expression and professional demeanor as before. As I gathered my thoughts I noticed once again the coolness of the air conditioned room and wished I had worn a sweater. I took a deep breath and began.

"I've tried to work at various jobs since I last saw you but because of my illness I've failed at most. I am currently employed at Sears but it is only two or three hours a day, a few days a week. Since I have schizophrenia I think I have limitations. I've learned that I can't overexpose myself. What I mean by that is I can only be actively involved with or around people for a few hours a day. Taking buses to work and being with co-workers is taxing. I find that I need time to be alone to recuperate. But when I am alone for long I get lonely."

I felt pressure to keep talking.

"I recently read a book on schizophrenia but a lot of it doesn't apply to me so I didn't find it very helpful. It appeared from this author's perspective that there are different ways to experience this illness. I still have auditory hallucinations, they come and go. They are like sounds directly outside my head but I can't make out what they say or mean."

At this point Dr. Hayes interjected.

"I suggest that we try Navane again. I know you've taken this in the past but it's worth another trial. Let's start with five milligrams a day and see how it goes. You can judge for yourself whether you benefit from it or not. There might be other things we can try if this is not helpful."

"I think that I also need medication to help me with my sensitivity to my environment," I said. "Normal everyday sounds like trucks going by or neighbors moving about and talking loudly in my complex make me feel as though I'm being bombarded. I can't find any peace and quiet. Also, I feel…I'm not sure how to describe this…I can't find a center of emotional gravity. It's like I'm without a mental backbone or an internal skeletal structure—like a jellyfish or a marshmallow. At times, I can only sit, immobile, unable to muster ambition to perform simple everyday tasks. Maybe a drug would give me strength."

"Are you—?"

I felt pressured to interrupt Dr. Hayes.

"At night I feel so much anxiety that I go to bed after supper. I'm not sleepy but am so frightened I try to find safety under the covers. Sometimes I just lie there staring at the ceiling. It seems like such a waste of time."

"Maybe Navane will help with the anxiety," Dr. Hayes said. "If not, we can try additional medication."

For the rest of the session we discussed how I felt at work and my involvement with the drop-in program. Eventually, I also told him about my new friends and of Don in particular.

"Our relationship is platonic. He's smart and can understand me in ways others cannot," I said. "We often meet at Burger King for pop and conversation. Even though he has schizophrenia he functions well enough to run his own business called DJS Enterprises. I think it has something to do with law."

When it was time for the session to end I silently concluded that I had made the right decision to re-enter treatment with Dr. Hayes. I stood and left. As I was walking away Dr. Hayes began writing.

> Since I have last seen Marcia there are certain notable differences. One is that she speaks freely of having schizophrenia and seems more accepting of her illness....She is able to separate herself from it [seeing it more clearly] in a way that she couldn't in the past....She has lost weight and is more spontaneous. Except for occasional contacts with staff and patients at the Mental Health Center, Marcia continues to suffer from some degree of social isolation—which is also a consequence of her living alone. She has a loss of interest in much of life....She continues to be hypersensitive and mistrustful in her relationships with others. Her thinking continues to be in some ways unrealistic and disorganized. She is quite sensitive to ordinary life stress, particularly criticism or harsh treatment at the hands of others. She is limited, it appears, in the amount of work she is capable of doing as the workplace causes anxiety and

headaches....Marcia continues to suffer from chronic schizophrenia and to have serious limitations.....

"Everybody gets depressed!"

"Marcia, that's what they said after I told them you felt bad and have been having a hard time functioning. So I said to them, 'But she's *clinically* depressed. That's different!'"

My sister, Bonnie, had phoned from Oklahoma to offer support. We discussed how it is difficult for me to communicate with my family, how most of the time we ended up quarreling. It would make me feel sick so I would try to avoid them for a while. I felt as though I needed people to be patient with me.

To borrow a metaphorical concept from Anne Lamott: When people are struggling to survive as in climbing up the side of a cliff with a thousand foot ravine stretching below them, they cling to whatever they can get their hands on and where ever they can place their feet and are not in the frame of mind for light conversation or playful banter. I felt that some of my relatives did not comprehend the depth of my difficulties or the extent of my struggles and because of this they failed to understand my inability to participate in cheerful talk. This made communication between us an ordeal.

"Do what you think is best," Bonnie said.

I changed the subject.

"I've applied for SSI again and was just re-approved for Section Eight housing assistance. There is a waiting list so I will need to wait a month or two before it starts."

"Let me know if there is anything I can do to help. I will always do whatever I can," Bonnie said.

"Thank you."

For the next few minutes we discussed the latest diet fads, jogging, and aerobics, then hung up.

Fall arrived and one day my negative mood completely overwhelmed me. While at work the depression grew so dark that I gave up and walked out of the store. I quit without a word to my supervisor and walked to the University's campus. Sitting on a bench by the river I watched people cross the footbridge near the Student Union. Plump ducks waddled onto shore pursuing bread crumbs and popcorn supplied by animal lovers. Others swam through the water stabbing at soggy morsels with their beaks.

I thought back over the last eighteen months of employment and felt I just couldn't do it anymore. I had found no joy in earning money. This had not been meaningful for me. No matter how hard I worked there was never enough of it. I was still in extreme poverty. There had to be more to life than mere survival, living hand-to-mouth, but I didn't know what. I couldn't fight the depression. After about an hour I returned home feeling once again a failure.

Within a few weeks the SSI payments began and, soon after, the housing assistance. I was grateful for the help. On most afternoons I continued to socialize at the drop-in center. I spent a lot of time dreaming of finding a husband and thought the best way to do that was to look as physically attractive as possible. I renewed efforts to bring my weight down but ate barely enough to keep myself nourished.

*

"Marcia, would you like to be a research assistant?"

Don and I were having one of our talks at Burger King as we sat in a booth on the second floor of the restaurant. Here and there students were eating and studying. Rock music came from speakers in the ceiling. Between sips from a giant glass of Pepsi he explained his proposal.

"My company, DJS Enterprises, is producing a book, the first of its kind in the field of law. Researched information will be used to impeach the testimony of expert witnesses for the defense in professional liability cases."

Don proceeded to tell me that his brother, an attorney in southern California, was his legal advisor and his brother's wife was his manuscript editor. He said he had two other people working for him, a woman who had wanted a part-time position and a friend with a J.D. (Juris Doctorate).

He had my attention.

"What would I do, exactly?"

"At the medical library located near the University Hospital you would use resource books to compile both biographical and bibliographical information on physicians. I've spoken with the head librarian and he's consented to our use of the library. I'll show you the medical directories as well as the Cumulated Index Medicus which contains volumes of medical literature listings."

"That sounds like fun!" I said. "I think I'd like to do that!" And I took a sip of pop.

Don was overjoyed; he smiled broadly.

"Thanks, Marcia! I'll pay you a fair wage. If there are some days when you don't feel well, just take a break for as long as you'd like. Keep track of your hours."

Don said that when I finished the work at the medical library he had some more I could do at the engineering library. I could research information to find negligence and liability in automobile design engineering as well as other things. This would be used to counter the testimony of defense witnesses in a court of law.

It was apparent that even though Don had a psychiatric illness with numerous symptoms, some of which were occasional grandiose ideas about his future, feelings of anxiety, and seasonal depression (he was despondent in the fall), he was still capable of running his own business—at least for the time being. His disheveled appearance gave the impression of disorganization; however, he was able to direct employees and manage complex financial affairs—which he did flawlessly.

"When can I start? Tomorrow?"

"Sure, come by my house in the morning and I'll give you a briefcase and go with you for the first day. I think you'll enjoy this project!"

My work at the libraries was, indeed, rewarding. I dressed in a skirt and blouse to appear professional. Don showed me the location of the books I would need and I completed the work, a process which took place over a period of several months. The finished book was entitled *JOURNAL ARTICLES and BIOGRAPHIES of DEFENSE DOCTORS and EXPERT WITNESSES* [Southern California Edition] Copyright 1985. The purchasing price was $150. As part of our work we found articles that doctors, engineers, and other professionals had written that contradicted statements they had made in court. Also, it turned out, many were not even experts; some had never been certified and some certifications had been canceled. This book was a key to the impeachment of their testimonies.

There was never a disapproving glance from anyone around me while I was in the libraries. For the first time in years I felt I had dignity and respect. Don's editor double-checked the accuracy of my information and later he told me about this.

"Not one error was found; it was perfect."

*

Why can't I find a partner? My mind was obsessed. It was a summer evening and I was sipping on a Bartles and Jaymes black cherry cooler. Just then the phone rang.

"Hi, Marsh! It's a boy! His name is Ryan. Seven pounds, thirteen ounces!"

My sister's excited and husky voice announced the good news.

"Way to go sis!" I said. "Are you feeling okay?"

"Yeah, I'm fine but it was a long labor. At one point I shouted, 'Give me a C-section or give me a gun!'"

"Meaning?"

"I couldn't take it anymore. And then the doctor said they had to do the C-section."

"Is the baby healthy?"

"He's doing great."

"I'm very happy for you."

"What are you doing now?" Bonnie asked.

"I was just sitting at my kitchen table drinking wine—I'm lonely and depressed. I feel horrible."

"Hang in there, Marsh. I'll be visiting Iowa City soon to show you the new baby, probably in a few weeks. I'll take you shopping. We can decorate your apartment. Remember, I love ya!"

"I love you too. And I'm anxious to hold Ryan. See you soon."

We said our good-byes. I continued drinking, then went to bed.

CHAPTER 15

I was alone, sitting on my bed in East Ward, resting, when two doctors in white lab coats entered my room. I learned one was a neurologist and the other appeared to be a resident in training. The balding senior physician addressed me.

"I'm Dr. Goldberg. I ordered the CAT scan you had yesterday. The results are unremarkable except for a small area of scar tissue above your left ear. Have you ever had a seizure disorder or convulsions?"

"No, I haven't," I said, thinking of my younger brother who had suffered from them most of his life.

"Then I see the slight abnormality as no reason for concern," he said and then turning, he left in a brisk professional manner.

The young resident started to follow Dr. Goldberg out the door but he hesitated and took a step back toward me. Leaning forward, I noticed an intense look in his eyes.

"Have you ever read *THE BROTHERS KARAMAZOV?*"

Taken aback, I quickly searched my memory then blurted out, "I've read part of it!"

In my teen years I had checked it out from the school library and read the first few chapters. I was puzzled by this sudden inquiry. The resident waited a few moments seeming to want more—an opinion or critique of the book—but said nothing. When I remained silent he turned and walked quickly out to rejoin the senior physician already moving down the hall.

This encounter had left me baffled and then I forgot about it. Now, years later, I recalled the resident's odd inquiry and took it for a prescription. I decided to find the book. It was summer of 1985.

Wild Flower Books, a frequent haunt of scholars and other University-affiliated people, opened at nine. One morning I headed downtown to the store, umbrella in my right hand and purse slung over my shoulder. Glancing at the dark clouds I felt keenly alert having finished my morning swim a few hours earlier. Nearing the building I noticed that the streets were sparsely populated. School was out of session. A wide window displayed novels by popular authors.

I walked directly to the information coral at the back of the store. A young man stood behind the counter arranging reserved books that sprouted little slips of paper at their tops. He became aware of my presence and spoke.

"May I help you?"

"I'm looking for the book with the title *THE BROTHERS KARAMAZOV*. I don't know the author."

He walked to the right expecting me to follow. Reaching a wall of books he pointed to a thick paperback.

"Those Russians go on and on—this one's over 700 pages and there are over a hundred translations in many languages."

As the man walked away I took the book from the shelf. Flipping through its chapters I scanned a few pages for clues to the kind of ideas that were presented: the Church; a man of culture giving the clergy a hard time; society and the criminal; without God, everything is permissible….The back cover said that Fyodor Dostoyevsky was one of the greatest Christian writers of all time. That in this story characters grappled with Christian theology and fundamental questions about life and death. He dramatized philosophical quandaries that arose from unavoidable ethical and spiritual choices.

For some reason I can't explain I closed the book and placed it back on the shelf. Walking a few feet farther down another author caught my eye: Alexander Solzhenitsyn. I'd heard of him. I pulled out *THE GULAG ARCHIPELAGO* and read the synopsis on the back: USSR prison industry; destructive labor camps; the soul; the end of Stalin....

Solzhenitsyn's literature reflected his beliefs that the basic problems of the Soviet Union and those that caused its downfall were primarily spiritual and moral. He attributed the loss of hope, demoralization, and high mortality to its atheistic culture.

Adjusting the shoulder strap of my purse I carried the book in my other hand to the opposite side of the store. I stopped before the shelf labeled PSYCHOLOGY. For a few moments I glanced over works covering various psychopathologies: anorexia, depression, anxiety, etc. My eyes fell upon *THE FAR SIDE OF MADNESS,* by John Weir Perry, near the floor. By examining the back cover and flipping through pages I briefly learned of some of his ideas. He had a holistic view of psychosis going beyond brain chemistry or somatic causes for mental illness. I thought I should look into this and put it in my hand along with the other.

As I continued walking along the aisles I heard muffled thunder. One last book caught my attention. I quickly grabbed it and rushed toward the cash register, hoping to reach home before rain fell. My final selection was about exorcism of the demonically possessed; a subject that intrigued me yet frightened me at the same time.

Having made my purchases I left the store into a torrent of rain. Under the cover of my umbrella I made my way to the bus stop. I thought I'd rather read than eat. I knew that with this expenditure my food budget would be strained. Thinking of how to economize I made plans to stock up on canned tuna and frozen broccoli which were to become the staples of my diet.

*

I felt my conscience nudging me to work again, at least to make an attempt. Being leery of paid employment I interviewed for a less pressured position as a volunteer at the city's public library. A week after meeting with the supervisor I started working three-hour shifts, two afternoons a week mainly checking in books and other library materials. I would have felt encouraged had any of the others working there initiated conversation or offered a smile but that was not the case. Volunteers were required to put in at least three months. Not being able to connect emotionally with anyone I was unable to finish and left disillusioned.

After a few weeks Ellen convinced me to try again. This time I helped with the Free Lunch Program for the homeless and other poverty stricken persons. Ellen, along with one other person, had just founded the program and I, along with other volunteers, began making and serving meals in a private club where we had use of the kitchen and dining area. I cut up carrots, potatoes, and onions, and mixed them in a kettle of boiling broth that also had chunks of donated beef. I put slices of bread and margarine on plates and placed them on tables. After patrons had eaten and left three or four of us cleaned up. I did this work on and off as I was able.

I continued to read books and I felt that my brain, once broken and unable to think well, was now being rebuilt with each word and concept I comprehended.

Next I sought help from a special employment agency whose aim was to find work for people who have a mental illness. It gave me a position in a coffee shop at the University's School of Social Work. My job was to stand behind a counter and serve coffee, tea, pop, and snacks to students, faculty, and staff.

Usually, in preparation for work, I took special care to look presentable. For example, one day I dressed in a deep red corduroy dress with a white turtleneck and styled my hair carefully. These things helped me to feel good about myself. But once at the coffee shop conversations were few which dampened my mood. I tried to smile at customers anyway and exchanged pleasantries.

One particular morning I served coffee to an energetic young student with a backpack over his shoulder. As he put a quarter on the glass counter and took the mug from my hand he thanked me.

"You're welcome," I said.

He walked a few feet toward an empty table then turned around.

"You don't *look* retarded!"

Apparently, he had been told that the former handicapped workers employed in the shop had been of limited intelligence and, therefore, so was I. I had to set him straight.

"Just because I have a psychiatric illness doesn't mean I'm retarded—and your use of that word is offensive to those with an intellectual handicap. It diminishes them."

"Oh, okay...sorry."

He looked confused but chose not to pursue the matter and sat down to study.

My immediate reaction to his ignorance was embarrassment and sadness. I wondered what all the people who visited the shop thought of me. I felt like I was on display. By being an employee here I was revealing to the world that I was disabled, that I was mentally handicapped. That set me apart from the rest of humanity. I became depressed. As a result of these thoughts a few days later I told my supervisor that I was quitting. I told her the main reason for this was the humiliation I felt. Her frown of disapproval disheartened me even more.

I continued going to the drop-in center. One winter day I met a man there about my age named Evan who would greatly influence my life for the next seven years. I had also seen him at the Unitarian Universalist Society where I had been attending services. He was reserved and kept mostly to himself. He always had a sad expression, his brown eyes on the verge of tears.

Throughout my trials of employment and volunteer work my heart had remained set on finding someone to love who would, in turn, love me. I had a need to be needed; something psychologists say is a basic human drive. In this frame of mind one evening I found Evan's number in the phone book and boldly made a first move. I called him at his parents' home where he had been staying. After several rings I heard a soft meek voice.

"Hello?"

"Hi, is this Evan? I'm Marcia. I met you at drop-in. Would you like to go out for hot chocolate? I could meet you at

Sonny's Café on Van Buren. We could talk and get to know each other."

Dead silence.

Finally, after a few moments and to my relief, he answered.

"Sure, I could meet you. When?"

"How about tomorrow evening at seven?"

"Okay, thanks. I'll be there."

I wanted to talk more but instead just thanked him and said I'd see him the next day.

The temperature that evening was below freezing. I eagerly walked into Sonny's and was grateful for its warmth. Small wooden tables were mostly occupied by college-aged people conversing. I took one near the frost-covered windows. As I nervously waited for Evan I noticed a green chalkboard listing an assortment of drinks and sandwiches. I had taken off my winter garb and hung it over the back of my chair. At precisely seven, Evan walked in. He came to the table and took off his coat.

"Hello," he said.

"Hi—cold night."

After Evan sat down across from me a waitress came and we ordered cocoa. For a brief moment I studied his appearance. He was wearing the same type of clothing I saw him wear every day at drop-in: an Oxford shirt with button-down collar; taupe Khaki slacks; brown leather shoes. He was tall and thin with curly hair and wore tortoise shell glasses. Overall, he appeared to be a thoughtful person, interested in intellectual pursuits.

"I hope you don't mind my asking…what brought you to the Mental Health Center?" I asked. "I heard you went to Yale. What happened?"

Evan lowered his eyes then looked up shyly and said in a barely audible voice, "Yes, I graduated from Yale. I then worked towards a Ph.D. in computer science at another university and that was when I got sick. I had gone out west to work in the artificial intelligence field for a while…it didn't work out."

"Yale is in Connecticut, isn't it?"

"Yes, New Haven."

I didn't think it appropriate for me to ask what his diagnosis was. That would be prying. But in order to keep the conversation going I found I had to ask other questions since he sat mostly still and seemed withdrawn.

I asked Evan if he enjoyed classical music and he said his favorite composer was Brahms. The waitress came over and set mugs on the table. We took a few sips. I told Evan that I had seen him at the Unitarian Universalist Society and he said he was a member. I brought up that I had heard that the UUS had a small discussion group that was meeting on a bi-monthly basis and asked if he attended that. Suddenly, Evan's eyes brightened and, previously slouched, he now straightened his posture.

"Yes! During the next meeting we'll be discussing Alfred Whitehead, his work."

"Who is he?"

"Whitehead," Evan said with a clear voice, "was a philosopher who phenomenologically examined the intelligibility of experience. His *magnum opus* was a book called *PROCESS and REALITY*. He lectured and wrote about such things as the hermeneutical metaphysics of propositions, metaphysics of creativity, philosophy of space and time, and philosophy of religion."

"Could you please explain something about his philosophy of religion?"

"Sure. He delved into questions concerning the self and its relation to the divine, such as, *Why does the world require God?* and *What kind of entity is God?*"

Feeling drawn I inquired as to when the discussion group would meet. Evan told me when and said he could give me a ride there. I gave him my phone number and address and we agreed to remain in contact.

My new friend became the center of my life. Evan was kind, sensitive and, most of all, brilliant. We shared a common interest in the UUS and I wanted to know more of what it stood for. So one day I visited its small library and checked out a book by Ralph Waldo Emerson, a philosopher and poet who is revered by many in the organization. I learned that Emerson had written on self-reliance, spiritual laws, love, friendship, intellect, idealism, something called the over-soul, and transcendentalism.

I looked up Unitarian Universalism as well. According to Webster, a Unitarian is a person who denies the doctrine of the Trinity: God the Father, God the Son, and God the Holy Spirit, three persons in one as in Christianity. Unitarians accept the moral teachings of Christ but reject the divinity and believe that God exists in only one person.

A Universalist is a person who believes in Universalism, the theological doctrine that all souls will eventually find salvation through the grace of God.

Periodically the UUS had dinners in its fellowship hall with guest lecturers speaking on controversial topics. I attended several and on one such occasion an astrophysicist addressed the fallibility of President Reagan's Star Wars Program. In the 1980's the president was enthusiastically promoting this expensive military project even though scientists like this speaker claimed that the program would fail and billions of dollars would be wasted.

My relationship with Evan grew and, eventually, he moved into my apartment. Even though I became less socially isolated my illness continued. I now found consolation in music, frequently playing Beethoven's *Moonlight* and *Pathetique* sonatas among others. While listening to music I found relief from my symptoms.

My sessions with Dr. Hayes were still helpful. Besides representing the scientific response to mental illness he was a source of stability that I found lacking elsewhere. Between meetings with him I would occasionally write him a letter, a progress report, or in some cases, a lack of progress report—whichever was the case.

Dear Dr. Hayes,

I am writing to inform you of my present situation. I don't see anyone for therapy right now. Occasionally, I talk to the supervisor of the drop-in program mainly to clarify my ideas and get feedback.

For at least eight years of various therapists and programs I have obediently followed orders to do this and that in an attempt to become well or at least try to get off Disability and SSI. Nothing has succeeded toward this goal. At the present time I think I know what is best for me and I will get to that shortly. So far, my mother supports me and my sister says, "You're an adult and can make your own decisions."

I presently still have these symptoms:
1. Soft auditory hallucinations often when I'm not playing music or when the TV is not on.
2. Quite often delusions—that I can feel people thinking about me and that I'm telepathic. (But once you said that since I know they're delusions, then they're not.)
3. Sleep disorder and exhaustion.
4. An inability to cope with the noise pollution in my apartment building—there is nothing I can do about it.
5. I am uncomfortable around 'normal' people in social gatherings. I feel different from everyone and I don't know what to say in conversations.
6. I am jumpy and easily startled.

I quit the job at Bill's Coffee Shop because I felt stigmatized. For eight years I've looked for a 'niche' in and out of the mainstream and now I realize I have limitations. At present, my work will be this (in my home):
a) When able, I will read for self-education to improve my vocabulary and expand my mind.
b) I will write essays.

c) I will strive to keep my appearance reasonably conformist and acceptable to society.

d) I will try to keep my apartment clean.

Although I am not employed right now I consider the aforementioned 'work.' I am not withdrawing or regressing in my opinion. We have tried several antipsychotics and antidepressants with little success….

CHAPTER 16

I spent less time at the drop-in center now that Evan was my companion. Since he owned a car, a red Datsun F-10 built in the late 1970's, we had mobility and thus freedom to travel. Over the next few years we went to concerts, theater productions and art institutes and museums as far away as Kansas City and Minneapolis. For the first time in my life I was free to drive to the grocery store where I shopped at my leisure.

Also broadening my scope of travel, Bonnie flew me to Tulsa about once a year for a marathon shopping spree to replenish my sparse wardrobe. We spent days at the malls and ate at nice restaurants. For a new look she'd take me to her hair stylist. Staying in her upscale home gave me a glimpse of how the other half lives and her lively extroverted personality lifted me—if only temporarily—from my usual somber state.

*

During the first summer after Evan and I began seeing each other, he, his parents, and I went to a Unitarian Universalist camp. This was my first vacation as an adult. The camp was located in northern Minnesota on an island. We stayed in a rustic cabin and gathered with other vacationers for programs at the lodge complete with a functioning fireplace and red-cushioned rocking chairs. The events of the week consisted of recreation and educational presentations given by experts in one field or another. We heard a nuclear scientist speak about the nation's latest military issues and weapons systems. I enjoyed our stay and found it somewhat relaxing. During this time my illness seemed to recede into the background and its symptoms troubled me little. But once I returned home the disturbances of mood and thought returned on a daily basis.

It was now August and I was scheduled to see Dr. Hayes. We had not met for several months. Once at the clinic I began to feel a sense of urgency and, as most times in the past, I also felt a sense of hope. As the session began I decided to explain some of the difficulties I had been experiencing. Making eye contact, I noted Dr. Hayes' expression was the same as always. He appeared to be listening but other, more important things, may have been on his mind. As a professor he did research, taught classes, and wrote papers and books in addition to seeing patients in the clinic.

"Since I last saw you I've been extremely irritable and impatient. The only exception was when I was on vacation. Other than that I have had a low mood and little motivation for everyday tasks. I think I need to distance myself from people."

I waited; Dr. Hayes remained motionless. I stirred in my seat, crossing one leg over the other, then reversing.

"Sometimes I explode over minor frustrations. I am often criticized and don't get much support from people. All of this is going on even though I have a new boyfriend. His name is Evan. We met last winter at the Mental Health Center."

As I paused Dr. Hayes interjected, "Do you see each other often?"

"We're living together now and get along well. We'd like to get married but if we did that I'd lose my medical insurance and I can't survive without that. He doesn't have a job with insurance to cover both of us. In fact, he's not working at all but is taking graduate courses at the University. I don't know if he'll be able to work in the future."

"What kind of diagnosis does he have?" Dr. Hayes asked.

"He has schizoaffective disorder. Could you tell me what that is exactly?"

"It is an illness that involves symptoms found in both schizophrenia and major depression. But it's more complicated than that."

I told Dr. Hayes I still had hallucinations most days though usually they were faint. Mainly I was seeking reassurance from him. I lacked confidence in my own opinions and ideas. Toward the end of the session I brought up employment again.

"I've been thinking I'd like to try to work again but because of irritability I'm afraid to. What can I do about this problem?"

"You are currently taking 4mg of Navane so I suggest you double the dose. If this doesn't help in ten days we'll try the antidepressant Norpramine. This drug should be taken with meals to help reduce nausea."

When it was time to go I bent over to pick up my leather purse and, after straightening, thanked Dr. Hayes for his help. He nodded and I left thinking the increase in medication might help. But it did not.

*

Having been interested in writing from a young age I enrolled in a University expository writing class in September. This became a struggle and once home from class the pressures of assigned work brought me to tears. However, over the next few months I completed all assignments and the instructor rewarded me with an 'A.' On the last day of class she also recommended that I try to get my work published. It would be several years before I ventured in that direction.

Evan's parents suggested that he and I move into a larger, two-bedroom apartment and so we did and we ended up using one of the rooms for a study. Bonnie bought me a Scandinavian cherry wood desk with matching chair. Evan purchased a Macintosh computer and taught me how to use it. I bought a filing cabinet for myself. The first day after bringing it home I spread folders out on the floor and labeled them for organizing and categorizing my writing. Evan told me he was impressed. We were fortunate to have two windows in the study which let in abundant sunshine, brightening the ambiance.

When not involved in school or household chores Evan watched television and I tried to read though I found it difficult to concentrate because of the TV. Evan spent so much time watching TV that I questioned Dr. Hayes about this. I asked why such an intelligent man would do so.

After thinking a moment he explained, "He's withdrawn."

Finally, Evan bought earphones that connected to the set so I could have some quiet but I felt his emotional absence even though we were in the same room. He was there, but he wasn't.

Still we enjoyed some times together, cooking nutritious meals from scratch and going to the University Field Campus, a wooded area near a lake. Evan took up sailing there and joined the University Sailing Club.

Evan and I were sitting one day at the kitchen table enjoying multiple cans of pop. Extending part way into the livingroom the table was a sturdy wooden structure I often scrubbed with Murphy's Oil Soap. We would talk and laugh about diverse things. For instance during one afternoon our new kitten, a long-haired gray Persian named Kingman came sauntering in and walked about eyeing the scratching post Evan had just set up. Suddenly, Kingman, in a flying leap, pounced on the post with all fours dug in. He clung briefly with ears pointed back, a wild look in his eyes—a mighty mountain lion, ferocious, fearless.

"He's got the concept!" Evan said.

"Way to go Kingman!" I said.

The kitten released his hold and landed on the carpet. He took a few steps, tucked his head under and laid down on his back, sprawled, legs relaxed, quite pleased with himself. I turned from Kingman to Evan.

"When I walk down the street I try to appear normal to fit in. You know—a steady gate, shoulders back—as though I have somewhere to go, which I usually do. But I always feel people may be thinking something's wrong with me."

An impish look came across Evan's face.

"Well...something *is* wrong with you!"

We laughed, aware of and, enjoying, our childishness. Pleasures for us were few; but at least, occasionally, we could amuse ourselves. I got up and walked to the refrigerator, took ice trays and filled our glasses. Opening it a second time I grabbed two more cans, placed them on the table and sat down.

"Evan...when are you the happiest?"

He thought a moment, filled his glass, and looked at me.

"When I'm engaged," he said.

*

When Evan was using his mind, engaged in intellectual pursuits, he was at peace. But sometimes during relatively tranquil days, psychic storms would erupt without warning. If he was under stress, feeling pressure from school or some other situation, he would have a psychotic episode of some kind. These spells could last from a few minutes to over an hour. Though he never lost complete contact with reality and always heard me when I spoke to him, he seemed not to have complete control. Sometimes weekly, other times less often, he would pace around the apartment in a rage, tormented by persons or ghosts from the past.

"Joel! I'm through with you!!" Evan would scream. Sometimes he would use obscenities, his face contorted in anguish and his eyes flashing hatred. Often, a fist flew through the air striking out at the enemy.

"How dare you insult me and denigrate my work! I'll tell you what you can do....!"

Nothing I said would calm him. And as I felt his pain I was also at a loss as to how to ease it. He suffered terribly and there seemed little I could do. Apart from these emotional outbursts Evan was saintly in his demeanor. He was an exemplary gentleman, a moral, ethical, kind and gentle soul.

One morning after receiving a phone call Evan announced exciting news.

"I've been invited to work for Dr. Nancy Andreasen!"

He explained that he and another computer scientist would create and analyze brain images on a computer.

"I start Monday!"

This was great. Andreasen, with an M.D. and Ph.D., had authored the book, *THE BROKEN BRAIN*, and was an eminent schizophrenia researcher working at the University. I learned from reading her book and from discussions with Evan that the primary aim of her research was to find a physical cause of schizophrenia. It was based on various hypotheses about neurochemical and/or structural abnormalities of the brain.

*

Western culture's scientific worldview—to which psychiatry belongs—had dominated my thinking during most of my adult life. As a Unitarian Universalist and secular humanist God and spirituality meant little to me on a day to day basis. Instead, I concentrated on what the world had to offer in the way of employment, intellectual growth and social relationships. With Evan employed in the field of biological psychiatry our discussions about mental illness came entirely from the scientific perspective. As years passed and I sought to recover from schizophrenia I continued to hold to the scientific view but, gradually, I began to see that more than biological, genetic and physiological factors needed to be considered. There were psychological, environmental and spiritual factors as well.

*

After Evan had been at his new job for a few months he and I volunteered to undergo tests as part of the research. We each had an MRI (magnetic resonance imaging of the brain) and neuropsychological testing. Afterward, the examiner told me that my MRI revealed normal brain structures and my IQ scores were above average. Knowing this boosted my self-esteem which had suffered since I had not finished college and had felt the fool for becoming involved in a cult. Anything that made me feel better came as a welcome relief from the low self-image I had accumulated.

In 1989, in addition to my sessions with Dr. Hayes, I started seeing a new therapist for counseling at the Mental Health Center. She was a social worker and a feminist. This counselor arranged for me to do volunteer work at the city's domestic violence shelter for women and children. I began by doing housework, cleaning bathrooms and the kitchen. As time went on my responsibilities increased and I ended up supervising the shelter during the night shift and answered the phone.

Most of the employees and volunteers there were feminists. During the four years (on and off) that I worked there I cut my hair short, read radical feminist literature, and returned to my smoking habit. I wasn't accepted by most of the others, many of whom were from upper-middle class backgrounds. There seemed to be distinct class boundaries. It was common knowledge that I had a psychiatric illness and as a result I was often treated as though I was inadequate and substandard. Once I heard someone in another room say, "She's crazy, you know! Don't believe anything she says!"

However, many of the lower class workers and residents were warm and accepting. Even though there were difficulties I appreciated the opportunity to work and feel useful. However, I eventually became emotionally and physically exhausted and had to resign.

Dr. Hayes suggested antidepressants on a regular basis which I would try for a few months then discontinue because of unpleasant side effects such as constipation, weight gain and feelings of emotional deadness. These effects outweighed the problem they were supposed to cure.

During my last years at the shelter I started to develop my spiritual life again and began to go to mass at a large Catholic church six days a week. I had stopped participating in the UUS because I felt drawn back to Christianity. Often, at home, I lit candles I had placed on a table that served as an altar where I prayed and listened to Christian music. I became interested in Mother Teresa, purchased books about her and her sayings and started working with the homeless women from a spiritual rather than a feminist perspective. I thought it wrong to wage war against men and, instead, began to see the need for transformation of both sexes. But as Evan and I started to develop relationship problems I drifted away again.

My behavior became increasingly erratic and chaotic. Most days I would impulsively follow this whim or that seeking instant gratification. I lived for the moment, had no goals and no purpose for my day to day existence.

Evan and I could now afford to be married but being ambivalent about our relationship and emotionally unstable, I married him in 1992 only to divorce him a year later. I then moved to an apartment on the other side of town and he moved to a house in an upscale neighborhood. Even though I suffered financially I sought something more than what Evan could give. But he was not to blame. His integrity was not in question; I just felt trapped and spent, my role as caretaker reaching beyond the limits of my abilities.

In times past to a small extent I had developed a mental mirror with which to observe myself, thereby gaining insight into my condition. But now that was gone. I found myself in a cloud of confusion with few friends and dwindling options. I saw less of my sister and was estranged from my family.

Without Evan and family ties my loneliness and isolation became unbearable. I sought a new companion but when the hope that sprang from that new relationship ended one winter night, I had a close encounter with death.

CHAPTER 17

One afternoon I was sitting on my couch wondering what to do. Behind me Renoir's *TWO SISTERS* with the caption *The Art Institute of Chicago* hung on the drab, beige walls. To my left was the stereo and headphones with stacks of CD's on nearby shelves. Kingman lay sleeping on the tan carpet remnant which partially covered the brown linoleum tiles.

I felt isolated and poured a fourth can of diet Pepsi, trying to think of someone to call. My sister had drifted away; Cedra, from drop-in, was the only girlfriend I had and she usually acted as though she didn't want to be bothered. Robert was working. He was the man I had started seeing after the break-up with Evan. He treated me as an equal.

"The mentally ill are people too!" he would tell others.

Shoulder-length wavy brown hair, a handsome bearded face, and wire-rim glasses, his looks captivated me from the start. And Robert was smart. I eventually called him my walking encyclopedia because I could ask him anything and he would usually have the correct answer. I had never dated a man with such strong character and colorful personality.

I put on my headphones and played Neil Young's latest, *Harvest Moon*.

*

It seemed a long walk to the convenience store. It was after 10pm. I went down the street oblivious to motorists and the extreme cold. At the store I took a bottle from the cooler and brought it to the cashier.

"A little wine for a fine evening?" he asked. I agreed and as I left he added, "Enjoy!"

Walking back to my apartment it seemed to take even longer.

The antique goblet was lovely—probably seventy-five years old or more. It was so fragile. As I drank the wine I took a few Stelazines and then some Tofranil. I drank more wine and took more pills. At one point I put Robert's belongings outside my apartment door. I tore his nieces' drawings off the refrigerator and let them float to the floor.

Over the years I had not found answers to problems that had plagued me and I had no hope for the future. I only saw the dull repetition of crippling psychiatric symptoms and inhumane treatment by society—the never-ending humiliation of schizophrenia. My attempts to find meaningful relationships had not been successful, leaving me feeling empty and abandoned.

Maybe it was the fear of dying, I don't know, but at one point I scrambled for the phone book and found Dr. Hayes' number. I realized I'd be waking him. His wife answered in a subdued tone.

"Hello?"

"May I please speak with Dr. Hayes?"

"Yes…just a moment."

He came to the phone. It was about 12:30am.

"Dr. Hayes, this is Marcia Murphy…."

From somewhere deep inside I felt a rising panic. I quickly explained what I had done and asked him what I should do. Not only did I realize I had no car but my sense of direction had begun to fade.

"What is your address? I'm going to call an ambulance," Dr. Hayes said in a steady voice.

I told him where I lived and soon an ambulance arrived and took me to the University Hospital Emergency Room. In the bright lights people seemed far away. A man in jeans, a physician, stood with his back to me. He was doing something with his hands and asked, "Why did you do it?"

"It's private."

That was it. Everything went black. I was gone. My medical record shows I had two seizures and went into a coma. At some later point I drifted back to consciousness.

I'm trying to talk to you! There is something in my mouth, going down my throat.

I plead with my eyes; I try to move my arms but they are tied down. I had been pulling IV's out so they had to use restraints. Looking from side to side I see Robert on my right, my mother on my left.

Please understand me—help me!

A team of physicians worked. One of them had called my mother who was listed as my next of kin at five Sunday morning. My mother called Robert. He brought what was left of my prescription drugs with him to the hospital.

They held a vigil at my bedside, waiting to see what would happen. Later, Robert said that I had so many IV's he wondered how they kept track of them.

A man was standing at the foot of my bed—one of the doctors. I heard him say, "I don't think she's going to make it."

A little later he said they had done all they could and that it was now up to me. I floated back into the unconscious.

Sunday passed and then, on Monday, I awoke. It was December 1993 and I was 39 years old.

*

With the suicide attempt I lost the spirit with which I had fought my illness. Someone even told me that since the attempt I was no longer brave. For the next six months my life was one of struggle and search for reasons to get up in the morning. Robert was like a locomotive—pulling me forward and motivating me to do what was required for survival which was all I could do. But I had little hope for my future and the medical community's answer to my depleted state was more drugs.

In January Dr. Hayes started me on a new antipsychotic called Risperdal and Paxil, an antidepressant. But after taking these for several weeks I still felt lifeless—dead. During days while Robert was at work I had only Kingman to keep me company and I began to use a newly acquired typewriter to write journal-like essays, recording my thoughts and feelings.

February 4, 1994

What is everyday life for me, a schizophrenic? I try to accomplish something but that isn't easy to do. The simplest tasks are quite a challenge. This illness has what are called "negative" symptoms. When these predominate I have absolutely no feelings. I enjoy nothing, not movies, music, friends, family, food, nor books. I observe others as though from a distance; they seem alien or from another realm. They appear to feel emotions and have passions; they have drive to accomplish many tasks. In my world, getting just a few things done each day is a source of pride....Being a person with mental illness I've had to make adjustments to life. For example, I would not be able to raise children. The crying of an infant would overwhelm me, even make me suicidal. But just as love and marriage help "normal" people enjoy life, they help people with mental illness enjoy more of life despite the hardship of living with a chronic illness....

And a month later:

Today, I began to function at 2pm. Life is chaos, without order. Nothing goes according to schedule. This is the life of a schizophrenic. Using an image Vincent van Gogh suggested, I feel like a bird in a cage and I am not free to fly. I am enclosed in a shroud of darkness—and it is cold....Surely there must be some joy. Show me the joy—where is it?

A couple of years later I came across the word *nihilism* and, looking back, I see that this term described my outlook during and after the time I stopped attending church, divorced Evan and almost killed myself.

Nihilism is a way of thinking that says one's life has no meaning or purpose. It is a thought system that says there is no absolute basis of knowledge or truth. It is a derivative of atheism, a co-conspirator of the godless philosophy.

My journal entries reflected an increasing emotional and spiritual hunger, an existential crisis. I was starving for reasons to live. I felt cut off from God, cut off from what the religious say is the source of life-giving energy and love.

*

In June I went to the clinic for my quarterly appointment with Dr. Hayes. Since I usually arrived ten minutes early I would take a *Noon News* from the receptionist's counter and read about current events and the weather forecast. Other times I just waited while staring at the modern art that decorated the walls.

Today Dr. Hayes appeared subdued as he approached. He paused twelve feet in front of me and nodded. I took this as my cue, lifted my bag from the chair beside me and proceeded back down the hall alongside of him.

"How are you today?" he asked.

"Fine, thanks. How are you?"

Once we were seated in his office I didn't waste any time. To his question of "How are things going?" I replied, "Five out of seven days are fair when I can function marginally but the other two days are horrible: I feel irritable and bitter; I have low mood and I feel completely overwhelmed by the smallest demands of daily life. On those days I can only manage to shower, dress, eat, and keep Robert, my boyfriend, company, for instance if he wants to go to a movie. I discontinued Paxil, the antidepressant, because it made me feel emotionally dead like others in the past."

"Would you like to try Prozac?" he asked. "It seems to help a lot of people."

"We did that a few years ago and I didn't like how I felt on that either so I don't want to try it again."

I preferred to try to think of ways to solve the problems which caused my depression, to get to the root, but Dr. Hayes never seemed to have time for that. Antidepressants were the quick fix, I thought, though there appeared to be a lot of scientific theories and happy people backing their popularity. At any rate, I dropped the subject and steered the conversation toward a topic of greater interest.

"Over the years I've done some writing and have a filing cabinet containing my essays and other projects."

I thought I detected a spark of interest in Dr. Hayes' eyes.

"What do you write about?"

"Issues and situations I've had to deal with in my life. So I'm writing from the perspective of someone with a psychiatric illness. I have piece for you. It's in here."

I leaned over my black Lands End briefcase/shoulder bag and pulled out an essay titled *What I Want to Say to the World.* I handed it to Dr. Hayes telling him the copy was his to keep.

We continued talking about various things and the session concluded after about thirty minutes. Toward the end Dr. Hayes brought up the subject of medication again.

"What is the current dose of Risperdal you are taking?"

"Four milligrams at bedtime."

"I suggest that we experiment with the dose. Trying it slightly higher as well as lower might be a good thing to do. Why don't you start by taking 3mg twice a day and phone me in a week or so to report the result."

I agreed to his suggestion and as I got up to leave he said, "See you in three months."

The essay I left with Dr. Hayes was as follows:

What do I want to say to the world? I want to ask the world to not hate me anymore. I am sorry I can't hold down a job and support myself. I am sorry tax dollars have to be used to support me. I am sorry I don't bathe enough and my hair is often messy. I am sorry my clothes aren't always clean and fashionable. I am sorry I don't look like other people and sit around a lot because I don't feel well. How others hate me for that! I am sad—depressed. There is little to inspire me and I don't feel motivated. I sleep too much. Then I overeat. And there is the caffeine.

Please forgive me because I can't follow your train of thought when you are speaking. You are talking too fast and I can't follow. Forgive me when my words come out jumbled and don't make sense. I wanted to be just like you but never will be. I wanted to go to college to learn and grow and get a degree. I want to say to people I work at such and such a place (I don't want to feel like a parasite). Why do you talk around me and not to me? Why don't you look into my eyes? Yes, I'm a human being too! Can't you look into my eyes when you speak?

Dr. Hayes liked what I had written and encouraged me to do more. This became a key factor in my improvement. But there would be others.

*

Finding the book *THE FAR SIDE OF MADNESS* had been completely serendipitous. At the time I had not been aware of its implications. Now I picked it up again and found validation for my growing belief that the experience of insanity, of psychoses in particular, might have deeper meaning than that promoted by modern psychiatry. As a result I began to move beyond biomedicine's framework for understanding to the trust in my own intuitions which were leading me in another direction.

I wrote an essay synthesizing Perry's views with my own and kept it to myself for a while. Then I shared it with drop-in members, publishing it in the center's newsletter. Lastly, I showed it to Dr. Hayes.

Perry says that neurophysiological manifestations of psychosis are not what the ill person experiences. Rather, it is the psychic phenomenon and subsequent turmoil, the emotions and thoughts that are experienced that deserve consideration. He sees the *psyche* (mind) and *soma* (body) as "indissolubly interwoven" and says that one should not be given more emphasis than the other. From his holistic perspective treatment should address both aspects of the illness: it should involve medications, but interpretation of the psychosis and its symptoms should play an important part as well.

During the time I was psychotic I heard demonic voices telling me there was no hope or meaning in life (nihilism) and that I should give up and kill myself. They cursed me and said I would go to hell.

In brilliant contrast a soothing voice in the rain had said, "Believe in Jesus Christ and you will be saved!" This message of light offered hope and direction. Now, cut off from God, with hardly enough energy to move, this light in the darkness pointed me to Christ. During the years since I'd heard the voice a faint notion had inspired me from time to time to heed the message but my employment and relationship challenges took precedence. I became absorbed in mundane pursuits.

One Sunday morning a week or so after an appointment with Dr. Hayes my mood was as low as ever.

"I think I'll go to church," I said to Robert.

We were sitting in the livingroom as sunshine poured through a large east-facing window. I sipped coffee as he downed a bowl of Cheerios mixed with Rice Chex.

"Really?"

"Do you think that's stupid?" I asked.

Pausing between bites he said, "No! Millions of people go to church! I don't think it's stupid."

After Robert finished his breakfast he left to visit his two children. He was a divorced dad and Sunday was one of the days he spent with them. I finished the pot of coffee then two liters of diet Pepsi before mustering the strength to dress for church. I had the motivation to shower but not to wash my hair. My clothes were plain: a baggy pair of black slacks, loafers and a lightweight beige tunic which required a camisole but I didn't own one. I hardly looked like church material but I walked out of my apartment anyway and headed down the street.

The closest Christian church was three blocks away. I wanted to go to the nearest one and didn't care about the denomination. As it turned out this one was Presbyterian. I walked through the doors and was greeted by a married couple as indicated by their name tags. They each shook my hand and smiled. I felt awkward but tried to smile back. As I approached the sanctuary I saw inscribed above the entrance way: *WHERE TWO OR THREE ARE GATHERED IN MY NAME, I AM THERE AMONG THEM.* I recognized Jesus' words.

Once in the sanctuary I walked to the right where twelve windows revealed a wooded area outside. The pews and decorative front portion of the church were oak and of a contemporary style. I sat down with the dozen or so others sprinkled throughout. Waiting for the service to begin I looked to the front wall where a ten foot high wooden cross with a gold ring around its center was displayed and at once felt an overwhelming peace. As hundreds more filed in, including the choir in burgundy robes, a pipe organ flooded the room with music. The bulletin listed the prelude as *In Green Pastures*, by Harold Drake. Just then someone went to the front and lit candles which sat on the ends of a long table (Presbyterians don't have altars). A large open Bible was at its center. Beautiful in its simplicity the whole setting called forth respect and a sense of awe.

I have to find answers. For many years I had been in a mental fog of uncertainty and, emotionally, it felt as though swimming through molasses. I had come to the church to find meaning in madness. My experience of illness, Perry's conjectures, my intuition and budding faith—these were the seeds. Now in this place with the hymns, prayers, and a sermon about building a personal relationship with a God who 'loves us more than we could ever imagine,' I felt as though my life was about to change. By choosing to follow the voice in the rain a new dimension of my life began to unfold.

*

C.S. Lewis, in *MIRACLES,* states that before one can decide if miracles can occur one must first resolve the philosophical question not only of their possibility but of their probability. This led me to thoughts about the different perspectives espoused by religion and science.

As many know, science and religion seem to have irreconcilable differences, differences that have existed for many centuries. Psychotic phenomena—for example, auditory hallucinations—are viewed by science as manifestations of brain abnormalities. Yet, I found literature from the religious perspective proposing supernatural causes. I thought that science, in its materialism, had negated the possibility of an unseen world and the impact it might have upon an individual. To me, it dismissed a concept without establishing proof.

William Lane Craig, author and research professor of philosophy, explains how it can be rational to believe in the supernatural. In the process of discussing an opposing view he quotes an atheistic philosopher, Michael Ruse, who said that according to the atheistic [or scientific] perspective, miracles [or supernatural events] are not repeatable—a necessity for verification—and, therefore, are 'outside of science.' Others view it as irrational to believe in the paranormal, that such beliefs lead to superstition and magical thinking.

Using the scientific method scientists attempt to prove or disprove hypotheses or theories. Therefore, to discount a proposed spiritual element without adequate proof is a misrepresentation of scientific method. There is much that science does not know. It seeks answers to questions of *how* but not of *why*. Craig states that supernatural occurrences need to be considered a possibility and, except in the case of a proven atheistic philosophy, investigators who do not consider this possibility show a closed mind.

In my desire to understand my illness and to recover, I was inclined to use analytical thinking. Much of my time was now spent in going to libraries. With intense curiosity, I sought out literature that delved into the possible connections between psychopathology and spiritual experiences. *Could there be a connection between the voices and mystical experience? Could there be religious meaning?*

The literature I found aided me in my search. And the more I looked, the more I found validation that psychosis can be purposeful in nature. Books and articles supported my view of it as an altered state of consciousness that can lead to mystical experience. This literature told me that there are others who go deeper than the materialistic view of psychosis and, because of this, I felt less alone. This discovery increased my confidence in the idea that the message I received in the rain was a religious communication facilitated by an altered state. The implications were far-reaching. *Was the Holy Spirit involved? And if so, what difference did His revelation make in the eternal scheme of things? How should I live my life from now on?*

CHAPTER 18

As I walked home from church my footsteps were infused with a subtle energy. Each step had more spring and I was no longer fatigued. The sunshine seemed brighter than before. For the rest of the day I felt more alive than I had in years. Sensing that Risperdal could have been a factor in my sluggishness, that evening I cut the dose from 6 to 2mg. The effect was immediate and the next morning I found my thoughts clearer and my mood, upbeat. My church attendance and lower dose of medication appeared to be a winning combination.

Within a few weeks I joined a prayer ministry, a small group of men and women who prayed for members of the congregation and for the world in general. The group met bi-weekly and encouraged individual devotions at home. This gave me the impetus to pray every morning. In solitude, I began to include my own requests along with those on the ministry's list. I asked God for healing—recovery from illness.

I also asked God what His will was for my life; this was another milestone. Throughout my life I had done what I wanted to do, I was my own boss. I was now starting to understand that God is the boss: He knows better than I the best course for my life. An all-wise God is bound to have the best plan. By September my life had changed so dramatically that I overflowed with good news for Dr. Hayes.

"I decreased the Risperdal to 2mg a day and I've become involved in a church," I said. "I'm focusing my life on

God and am doing better now than I've ever done in my life. I feel energetic and my mind is clear. Looking back, my life seems to have been one of chaos. I had little control over what I did and I didn't understand that I should take responsibility for my actions rather than act on impulse. I've been praying about this."

What I believed at the time but didn't verbalize to Dr Hayes was that, as I focused on God, my everyday decisions were now anchored in a new reality. This spiritual reality was life-affirming and strengthening. Researchers refer to this stabilizing affect (less impulsiveness and more volition) as the 'internal locus of control.' Paradoxically, my newly acquired self-control was the result of submitting to God's will, thus giving up my own.

With my fingers, I manipulated a metallic sculpture sitting on the table beside my chair. Its tiny scale-like movable pieces held together by a magnetic force conformed to my design. Dr. Hayes looked like he expected me to continue so I stopped and gave him my full attention.

"Recently, I signed up for two part-time volunteer jobs. I also do a lot of reading, something that has been hard to do for a while. At times, I still struggle to have an interest in things but I find books on religious topics hold my attention. I also do housework and cook meals."

"How do you sleep? You've had problems with that," Dr. Hayes asked.

"Sometimes I only get about four hours at night. Maybe you could prescribe something to help me sleep."

"It sounds like you are hypervigilant. Trazadone is a medication that could help. It's an antidepressant but is also used for sleep."

I agreed to try it.

Before it was time to go I brought up the concern that I would someday like to try paid employment again.

"I'd like to have a real job but don't feel able at this time. But even if I did it might cause me to lose my medical insurance and ability to pay for medication which I can't live without."

"Why don't you stick with the volunteer work for a while and see how that goes."

Dr. Hayes seemed encouraged by my progress and gave a rare smile as I turned to go. It wasn't often, I'd heard, that a breakthrough occurred in the treatment of schizophrenia. No doubt his job had brought him many trials as he tried to help those with few prospects for recovery. Though I was not fully restored, the changes that I had just experienced were reasons for hope.

> Today, Marcia looks quite good and has a bright smile. She is not very spontaneous but is certainly logical and goal-oriented in her conversation. She shows little outward sign of distress….Her residual schizophrenia manifests itself in some lack of interest and motivation, but she manages to do volunteer work and things in the home. However, something that is important to her and captures her interest is her religious faith and participation in her church. These things she finds meaningful. She prays a good deal and one of the things she prays about is that she not be as impulsive and stay with things more than she has in the past. At any rate, she looks well and appears to be doing very well indeed.

CHAPTER 19

I soon learned of a weekly women's Bible study held at my church which I decided to attend. It was here that I heard not only what I believed to be God's word, but also found friendship. This was to become a source of spiritual strength, a strength that would keep me going forward in times of hardship.

*

The Christian religion is based upon the person Jesus Christ. Born approximately in 4 B.C., Philip Yancey states (again from *THE JESUS I NEVER KNEW)* that He came from a family of humble circumstances: *without power or wealth, without rights, and without justice.* Being a Jew, He lived in a hostile environment under oppressive Roman rule.

Many believe that Christ has influenced the world more than any other person. Though hung on a cross in apparent defeat, His death and resurrection were the beginning of a new order in which light triumphs over darkness.

Christ lived a life at odds with the world's ways. His concern was for the poor, the meek, and disadvantaged, whereas the world venerates the rich, beautiful, and strong. Christ stressed loving one's neighbor, not competing. He stressed setting the heart not on the accumulation of material goods but on developing qualities of character, thus offering a counter-perspective to philosophical materialism.

Yancey states that Jesus' example revealed a God who *knows no undesirables.* Through His miracles, healing of the sick and lame, feeding the hungry, and care for the outcasts, Christ showed that everyone is important to God. Yancey believes that in a world where selfishness and decadence dominate human motives, Jesus brought justice and righteousness.

Christ was rejected by the world. People who have a mental illness have also been rejected. But Christ brought hope to the sick, poor, and downtrodden. Many Christians strive to imitate Him and, in doing so, reached out to me.

At the women's group I had the opportunity to set up things for coffee and sometimes clean up later. These activities helped me to feel that I was contributing—in this case to a faith community. My work not only helped others, so was inherently valuable, but increased my own sense of worth.

The cult had exploited members, but I found my Christian church had as its foundation the belief of serving God and one another in love. Some travel to Third World countries to set up schools, and medical and dental clinics. Young people work at cleaning and re-building low-income inner-cities. Others work in church-run secondhand stores to provide relief for the poverty-stricken and still others risk their lives by promoting peace in war-torn global communities. Many have been internationally recognized for their conflict resolution skills.

The Christian church became for me a positive influence, giving back to me some of what I'd lost in the cult. As a result of my years in the Unification Church I had lost not only my feeling of self-worth, but also my very sense of self. Brainwashing empties the mind and fills it with the leader's thoughts and agenda. Through this process my personality was nearly destroyed and, with it, my self-determination. Now, as my Christian faith grew, my sense of a new self and mental control grew. I started to receive healing from my cult ordeal and found a new identity as a child of God.

The drop-in center acquired the name of Clubhouse. I became editor of their monthly newsletter and using the center's old IBM computer I compiled essays, poems, and artwork submitted by Clubhouse members. This also gave me the opportunity to publish things of my own. Though I had failed at employment, writing brought success and showed me that I could put rational thoughts down on paper thereby developing my intellectual skills. This sense of joyful accomplishment gave impetus for going forward and to strive for other victories.

My writing dealt with the relationship between medicine and spirituality beginning with short essays on a variety of mental health topics. One specifically dealt with faith and healing in which I said that having faith in God and being part of a religious community enhances a person's health.

Physicians need to be aware of the strong association between religious faith and health outcomes in patients. The implication for psychiatrists is that they can improve treatment for people who have a mental illness by integrating spiritual issues and discussions into the traditional behavioral and pharmacological ones currently in use. Science and religion should not be compartmentalized as if they are different and unrelated parts of human existence.

In another which I titled, *Blameless?*, I wrote that just as there are good and evil people in the general population, there are both good and evil people with mental illness. And in the case of people who have a mental illness who commit crimes or violent acts, I didn't think that their diagnosis of mental illness should always be used as an excuse.

In one essay I expressed my view that most people with mental illness can decide whether they want their mental health to improve or not and, in the act of choosing, can further determine whether to learn and grow or retreat into resignation and stagnation. While it is true that some with serious mental illness seem to be stuck in a netherland of madness—out of touch and hopelessly beyond reach—I still believed that the human will gives everyone a degree of freedom, enabling people to make decisions however fragile they may be.

*

It was a hot and humid summer day. I arrived at the clinic for another appointment with Dr. Hayes. Once seated in the crowded waiting room I burrowed into my shoulder bag, found a Kleenex, and wiped the sweat from my brow. The air conditioning felt good. I glanced around to see if I knew anyone there and was disappointed when I did not. Still, I sat in anticipation of a productive meeting. Dr. Hayes was supportive and today I had something exciting to tell him. At precisely 1pm he appeared. As usual, we took our seats in his office.

"I'm getting along well," I said clearly. "I have an article that was just accepted for publication!"

I told Dr. Hayes that a paper I wrote was accepted by the *Schizophrenia Bulletin*, a professional psychiatric journal and that it would come out in one year. My article was titled, *FIRST PERSON ACCOUNT: Meaning of Psychoses.* In it, I said that science and religion should be considered compatible with respect to the problem of psychoses. To speed recovery two aspects of psychiatric disorders needed to be considered: theories of neurochemical brain dysfunction and spiritual questions regarding the meaning of illness. I explained how both medication and religious faith had contributed to improvement in my condition. My aim in writing was to encourage psychiatric professionals to take a broader look at psychotic phenomena, e.g., hallucinations, and to consider the devastating impact psychosis may have on those who've experienced it.

Dr. Hayes congratulated me and encouraged me to keep writing. He also gave me suggestions of other topics that might be explored. Then the discussion turned to medications.

"I'm taking 3mg of Risperdal daily but I've quit taking the Trazadone. For over a year I'd been having awful nightmares, it seemed like several times a week. As a result I hadn't been getting enough rest and felt tired during the day. I always thought the schizophrenia caused it then one afternoon at Clubhouse I asked a supervising counselor if Trazadone could cause terrifying dreams. He said it could, that nightmares are a known side-effect, though uncommon. So right away I quit taking it. As soon as it was out of my system I stopped having nightmares."

Dr. Hayes acknowledged my discovery and supported my decision. I tried to cut down on caffeine to help me sleep. Risperdal had a slight tranquilizing effect so that helped.

I told Dr. Hayes that I continued to publish the newsletter at the Mental Health Center and showed him copies. I told him that Robert and I had decided to stop living together though we remained friends. I also said that I occasionally had a recurrence of brief periods of depression but wanted to learn how to cope with those and felt that being active in church helped.

Glancing at my Timex I saw there were only a few minutes left in the allotted half-hour. In summation I said, "I believe there are three things that are responsible for my present level of functioning: Risperdal, having new friends, but most important of all—my faith which is becoming central to my life."

Dr. Hayes turned in his swivel chair and picked up a pen.

"I'm glad things are going relatively well. I recommend that you continue with the present dose of Risperdal. Do you need a new prescription?"

I said, yes, that I did. He quickly wrote one out and handed it to me. After thanking Dr. Hayes I left, stopping at the receptionist's counter to schedule my next appointment.

> Marcia reports that she has been getting along satisfactorily. She looks well today, smiles easily. She indicates that, generally, her mood is satisfactory and that she continues to be strengthened by her religious faith. She volunteers at church and says she finds this rewarding. I continue to feel she has done much better since being on Risperdal, however, during this same period she has had a strengthening of her faith. She commented that when she gets depressed occasionally, she thinks it situational and made a list of factors that she thinks cause low mood.

They include times when church Bible study and prayer groups do not meet. It is nice to hear her feeling this sense of belonging and missing activities of that kind, but her point was that we need to pay more attention to these factors and how to cope with them rather than using antidepressant medication. I think she is doing rather well.

Not long after my appointment with Dr. Hayes I had a dream which had a strong impact on me and strengthened my resolve to continue along the spiritual path I had chosen.

It was night with strong winds blowing and thunder and lightening. I was in a body of dark water—a deep lake or an ocean—and I couldn't see the shore. What was keeping me afloat was a large cross. As turbulent waves tossed me about, my body lay partially over the top of the wooden beams and I clung to it. The cross was giving me life in the midst of a storm and I would not drown as long as I kept hold of it.

This experience was to be one of many that in future years convinced me there was a reality which transcends the material world, a reality I thought I must heed.

*

Dr. Hayes referred me to a book by Anton Boisen, *THE EXPLORATION OF THE INNER WORLD*. Boisen wrote that there is a certain relationship between certain kinds of mental illness and religious experience both of which he sees as attempts of nature to heal and transform the individuals involved. Where the outcome is inner victory the label 'religious experience' is given; but where the outcome is inner defeat the result is often 'insanity,' leading to further deterioration. The implication is that spiritual battles take place within individuals who at some point choose whether to align themselves with the darkness or the light. Our pastor arrived at a similar version of this delineation. One Sunday during a sermon he exhorted, "It's either Christ or madness!"

Many people think of the Christian church as a place of rules and regulations. I, however, have found it primarily to be a place of healing and restoration. My search for the connection between faith and healing was aided with the definition of terms. According to the *HANDBOOK of RELIGION and HEALTH* by Koenig, McCullough, and Larson:

> The word 'healing' comes from the Greek [Correction: German] word *heilen,* which means 'to become whole,' 'to set right,' or 'to restore.' 'Religion' comes from the Latin word *religare,* which is composed of two roots, *re* and *ligare. Re* means 'back' and *ligare* means 'to bind, bind together.' Thus, the word 'religion' literally means 'to bind back together'…the word 'religion' itself involves a description of healing. Health, religion, and healing all have the common theme and task of making the person whole, sound, transforming him into a state of optimal well-being—restoring the person, both mind and body, to order and balance….

CHAPTER 20

It's reductionistic. It's simplistic.
Such were my thoughts in early 1997 as I wrote *Psychiatric Illness from the Religious Perspective,* a paper designed to promote spirituality in medicine. I used a combination of personal account and theory to describe the transformative impact of my psychosis. I said that, standing alone, the biomedical model of psychiatric illness is reductionistic in the sense that human beings are viewed as machines. This model may have some advantages—helping to generate effective medical treatments like antipsychotics—but it has limitations and may lead to misunderstanding. Instead, I favored a holistic view of mental illness that merges secular psychiatry and religion. Such a view would show that the mind, body, and spirit are interrelated. I describe how this perspective had brought healing to my life.
My experience and that of my friends had been that psychiatric professionals imposed their materialistic perspective on their patients through scientific interpretation of mental phenomena. For example, instead of helping to solve the patient's personal problems—seeking the underlying root causes of depression—doctors often prescribe antidepressant drugs. Granted, at times medications may be called for. But it still appears to be the case that the quick fix of using a drug, which saves time, is too hastily administered. And although with medication an elevation of mood may temporarily ease

distress; the social, psychological, and spiritual conditions which have caused sadness remain. One friend had even been told by a health care provider: "*Chemicals* are the foundation of existence!" Prompted by statements like this I hoped to show in my writing that there is a spiritual aspect to existence as well as the physiological.

One day in April of 1998 at a session with Dr. Hayes he expressed agreement with the holistic perspective by saying, "I think schizophrenia, like most mental illness, is influenced by many factors—there is not a single cause. At various times emphasis has been placed on some factors while others have been neglected due to prevailing theories or new discoveries."

Over the next few years I continued to explore in my reading and writing connections I saw between religion and medicine, specifically psychiatry. Drawing upon my own experiences I wrote and published articles which I hoped would provide insight into what it is like to have a serious mental illness that affects all aspects of one's life.

*

Robert leaned back in his brown leather Eames chair and put his feet up on the matching footstool. It was his usual resting spot after a hard day's work. I had come over for a visit and sat nearby on the navy-striped couch. As usual, I had a diet Pepsi on the end table to my side. With the twenty-year-old Magnavox we watched the Cubs verses the Braves, two of our favorite teams. It was the top of the 7th and the Cubs had just gained another run.

Robert muted the set and going over to the stereo put on Andrea and Giovanni Gabrieli's *A Venetian Coronation 1595*. We thought baseball and late renaissance music a delightful combination. I turned to Robert as he commented, "I wonder who will hit the most home runs this year."

I sometimes asked him deep questions while he was distracted by sports on TV and such. Usually, though, he welcomed my questions.

"I hope you don't mind if I change the subject but I want to talk about similarities between mystical experiences and psychosis. I've read in books and have seen on TV that when Native American Indians smoked or ate plant substances—you know, when they did this in centuries-old religious rituals—that they actually became psychotic. But weren't the Indians trying to have spiritual experiences like visions and other things like that?"

Robert turned from the game and said, "They were. But even now in current times in places like northern Mexico, Arizona, and New Mexico, it's legal for them to use mescaline which is a psychedelic drug. It comes from a type of cactus. There are other derivatives they also use. Indians have gone into the desert searching for spiritual enlightenment. They fast and use plant substances to bring on visions and whatever else might come to them."

Robert went on to say that some of these substances are in a strong drink they concoct. Often it causes vomiting but, even so, it can send them into a different plane or realm of consciousness. He said there are other hallucinogens that have similar effects such as marijuana. But he thought marijuana opens a person up in a milder way.

"I think hallucinogens can be dangerous!" I said. "I've heard of people having—

"Bad trips?" Robert nodded. "That can happen! Some people go insane and never recover."

I continued.

"This helps me see how neuroleptics or antipsychotics fit in. Just as drugs like mescaline and marijuana open a person to altered states there are psychiatric drugs that restore them to reality, the reality known as sanity."

I reached for the dictionary from under the table. Psychiatric medications are sometimes called 'psychotropic' so I wanted to see how this was defined. Opening to Webster's definition I read it to Robert: *Having an altering effect on the mind, as tranquilizers, hallucinogens, etc.*

"Both tranquilizers and hallucinogens are in the same category," I said. "LSD was popular for a while. What does that stand for?"

True to his encyclopedic manner, without hesitating, Robert said, "Lysergic acid diethylamide. A Swiss chemist discovered it in 1938. It's a very powerful drug."

I asked if he knew of other hallucinogenic plants and he explained that there are mushrooms that contain psilocybin that can cause hallucinations. Many are found in the Pacific Northwest but also in other parts of the world such as South America.

I told Robert that I had met a few people who had schizophrenia at Clubhouse who had gotten ill during illegal drug experimentation. I thought I saw some similarity between the 'hippy' culture's mind-altering trips and the altered perception of schizophrenic psychoses.

*

In Stanislav Grof's *REALMS OF THE HUMAN UNCONSCIOUS* he talks about changes in the mind produced by psychedelic drugs, changes which may involve hallucinations, delusions, extraordinary sensory perception or different states of awareness. Grof states that the psychedelic experience brought about by LSD is 'phenomenologically indistinguishable' from that of religious mystics recorded in sacred texts and scriptures from ancient times. He said that some experiences involved mystical unions with a divine source and others consisted of horrifying encounters with demons.

I found more about hallucinogenic plants and mysticism in *THE ROAD TO ELEUSIS: Unveiling the Secret of the Mysteries* by Wasson, Ruck, and Hofman, the chemist who discovered LSD. And there was other literature as well.

*

Based on this discussion it is evident that psychedelic drugs alter the mind in ways not totally understood by scientists or religious mystics. In humans, who consist of mind, body, and spirit, chemicals may play a part in religious and hallucinogenic phenomena, but to say that they are the *source* of such experiences is a misattribution. Though the part they play may be significant other factors are also involved.

Consistent with my search for meaning I sought similarities in mystical states and pathologies of the mind. I came to believe that the old maxim seems applicable: science answers questions of *how* things work in the physical world, but questions of *why* must be left to the theologians. Theories about chemicals in the brain do not explain the content of hallucinations. This explanation comes from elsewhere. When this is answered does this point to the source of the phenomenon? It depends on how the problem is defined. That definition determines the way one sees the source and definitions vary with each worldview.

Faced with the materialist or religious worldview, I opted for the latter. And having done so, I came to believe that the voice I had heard in the rain was God's and, with this, my life was turned around. I then sought validation for my belief in a supernatural reality that would take into account a divine source. I hoped to find people who might affirm my belief that I had had an encounter with the Almighty.

CHAPTER 21

"You came up against a powerful force!" Dr. Hayes said. We had been discussing my experience in the cult. It was clear from the aftermath that this experience had been an important factor in my mental breakdown.

A word is an expression of a thought or idea. Thoughts and ideas come from an intelligence. Intelligence comes from a mind and a mind from a thinking being. I believe that the hellish and divine voices came not from within my own mind but from without—from other sources.

Carl Gustav Jung was a depth psychologist who considered phenomenological studies and religious interpretations of psychotic episodes valuable. He found meaning in the content of hallucinations. In *MEMORIES, DREAMS, REFLECTIONS*, he described his own experience of a 'haunting' during which he heard voices while in his home. He labeled these as 'parapsychological phenomena.' Gregory Zilboorg, in *FAITH, REASON, and MODERN PSYCHIATRY*, says that "there is more than mere suspicion that the scientist who comes to ask metaphysical questions and turns away from metaphysical answers may be afraid of the answers." Jung was not afraid of metaphysical answers or extraordinary interpretations of mental phenomena.

As a naïve teenager I was attracted to the supernatural. At slumber parties I played with Ouija boards and experimented with levitation. Later in life I heard Christian speakers denounce these "games" as dangerous. They warned that such practices were "a means of tapping into dark forces we cannot control."

Mainstream psychiatry labels supernatural explanations as "delusional thinking." In September 2000 I discussed in a quite rational way the spiritual approach to understanding psychosis with someone who holds a Master's of Divinity degree, the Associate Pastor of St. Michael Presbyterian Church where I had become a member. I wanted to know the truth about the "voices."

William James, in his *VARIETIES of RELIGIOUS EXPERIENCE,* has said that "primal truth should be the core and foundation of beliefs" and that "the origin of the truth would be an admirable criterion....The history of dogmatic opinion shows that origin has always been a favorite test...." The Bible had become my origin of truth and the basis for interpretation of my psychotic episode.

I sought Pastor Reinhart's help in bringing together my experience of psychosis and the spiritual perspective of the Bible. I was hoping that in the course of our discussion I could find an explanation for the extraordinary reality I had perceived. I was aware, however, that this explanation would not hold value for those who deny the existence of God or who have excluded religion from their worldview.

Pastor Reinhart was aware that I had experienced a mental illness and had read some of my writing pertaining to this topic. He agreed to meet with me one afternoon. I arrived at his office carrying a bag of books supportive of my view. I stacked them by my side after I sat down.

Sitting across from Pastor Reinhart I noticed on the corner of his desk, a miniature waterfall trickling over a metal sculpture. He appeared to be a man of order as his books, papers, and assorted objects were neatly arranged. Next to his desk was a large window that let in ample sunlight and to one side was a long counter with a running computer, the screensaver busy at its task.

Even though Pastor Reinhart's wavy blond hair casually swept back gave the impression of youthfulness, he had a strong presence. I saw in him a man of integrity and uncompromising faith.

Our conversation was informal and proceeded in a relaxed manner. To begin, I took two pieces of paper from my shoulder-bag and handed them to him.

"Here are charts showing spiritual experiences that are described in the New Testament. There are literally thousands having to do with angels, demons, the devil, miracles, visions, healing, and so on. The charts are from the appendix of Morton Kelsey's *ENCOUNTER WITH GOD*. Are you familiar with his work?"

"Yes, I've seen some of his writing."

"For those who value religion these references confirm that spiritual forces and experiences exist. They have been present throughout history and continue to influence our lives today. Given the biblical perspective I'd like to hear how you interpret mental illness. But before you start let me say that many people with mental illness I've spoken to feel as though they are being attacked by evil spirits and that the voices they hear represent forces bent on their destruction. So I'd like to ask you, are there any situations of this kind in the New Testament? What about the story of Jesus who after going into the wilderness was 'tempted by Satan'? It says that Jesus rebuked him and then the devil 'left Him until an opportune time.'"

After Pastor Reinhart laid the pages of references on his desk he turned squarely to face me.

"With Jesus we're talking about the Spirit, actually God's spirit, compelling Jesus to go into the wilderness which, biblically, is a place of trial. In other words He is laid bare to struggle with evil. So on one level the battle is God-willed. Yet the source is the evil one. God does not protect Jesus from the evil one. What we see is really a decisive battle and Jesus is, through the power of the Spirit, victorious in that battle."

"So it was something that had to be done? It was part of His mission?" I asked.

"Yes. I think it was a decisive and purposeful encounter that Jesus had with the evil one in which He showed himself to be true to God. And one of the implications for our conversation may be that Jesus' encounter with the evil one was not an indication of His disobedience or failure, but part of the human experience."

I glanced over at my stack of books.

"So would you say it is part of the human condition that people have to battle such forces in their lives? Perhaps people with mental illness have extreme experiences because they are in touch with spiritual things or maybe they have fallen into conditions that allow dark forces to invade their lives by something they have done."

Just then I reflected back on some of the Ten Commandments found in the book of Exodus: *You shall have no other gods before me....You shall not make for yourself an idol....You shall not bow down to them or worship them....*

Clearly, in my worship of Moon I had disobeyed God's laws, thereby venturing into occult realms. Maybe this had created conditions that allowed dark forces to invade my life.

"Certainly, all of us may experience battles," Pastor Reinhart said, "but I'd be careful in talking about those who—I think you said, 'made themselves vulnerable'"

"Have done something to allow evil to come into their lives," I said.

"I think that sometimes this is so, that we can walk down a path for whatever reason, not always a self-chosen path—

"Do you mean, for example, when children are victims of abuse and then become mentally ill although they were innocent? The children had no control over what occurred when they were dependent on their parents," I said.

"Yes," Pastor Reinhart said, "and that's where sin invades the human condition and because of this we may become genuine victims. I think that is certainly true. And sometimes, as a result of our choices we find ourselves more open to spiritual attack as you say. Certainly, it is recognized in the literature that through the use of mind-altering drugs—hallucinogens—we may make ourselves more vulnerable. So, yes, I think spiritual battle can be a reality in our lives but it is not always self-chosen."

"I agree. Have you heard of *THE HANDBOOK for SPIRITUAL WARFARE* by Ed Murphy? Using a strong theological foundation Dr. Murphy tells how we may gain victory in spiritual conflict."

"No," Pastor Reinhart said, "I'm not familiar with that one."

"The traditional psychiatric stance," I said, "is that such a viewpoint—the very concept of spiritual battle—is delusional. But Dr. Murphy is not mentally ill; he is a well respected professor and leader in worldwide missionary outreach."

"The Bible certainly gives accounts of spiritual warfare, not only in the example we used with Jesus earlier. There's also Ephesians: 6."

Pastor Reinhart picked up his Bible and searched the pages until he found the passage.

"Here it is, verse 12: *For our struggle is not against flesh and blood, but against the powers of this dark world and against the spiritual forces of evil in the heavenly realms.* That's why we need Christ. In Colossians 2:10 it says that *Christ...is the head over every power and authority.*"

"That's one of the many areas in which the other world religions fall short," I said. "Not only do they not adequately address the problem of evil, its origin and influence, but they fail to give victory over it. Christ, alone, does that."

Pastor Reinhart nodded.

"Many will call Christ a great moral and ethical teacher but these same people will say that Christ is lying when He claims to be the Son of God. This is a contradiction. Great moral and ethical teachers are far more likely to tell the truth."

"I agree," I said. "And the idea that all religions are equal doesn't add up. This concept is put forward by those who have not studied the world's religions. For if they had they would see that the major religions are exclusive, for the beliefs they each represent cancel out or contradict the beliefs of others. I learned a lot about this from books written by Josh McDowell. He says it is impossible for the different teachings to be true at the same time which brings us to the exclusivity of truth itself.

"To say there are multiple and contradicting truths is relativism which then makes truth subjective, which by definition is impossible. For truth to be truth it has to be objective, independent of human opinions—originating elsewhere. To say humankind is the origin in the subjective sense is to deify humans...."

We went on to discuss a variety of biblical stories. First, the instance in 1 Samuel 16, where King Saul was bothered by an evil spirit. Many people have interpreted this to mean Saul was mentally ill. We talked about Job's suffering and Amos' prophesies, all of which had to do with calamity of one sort or another. Then I brought the conversation back to modern day circumstances and Pastor Reinhart expressed his opinion on the orientation of psychiatry in the United States.

"Because modern psychiatry views psychosis as primarily a physical disorder it is blind to treatments that are more holistic in nature."

He had touched upon an important point and I was quick to respond.

"Do you think there may be value in psychotic episodes? Do you think it is important to consider the *content* of hallucinations?"

"Absolutely. It makes sense to pay attention to the content, especially to the questions it evokes, the search that it may prompt. For example, when you experienced an evil onslaught—

"I felt attacked. Psychiatrists I've had have mostly ignored what my illness might mean and, instead, focused on the use of medication. But when I started thinking about this from a religious viewpoint it changed my life."

"There are probably instances as well," Pastor Reinhart said, "of people who've had similar battles but didn't weather them, that were in a sense destroyed by their experience. Maybe these episodes determine what's going to happen later on in the person's life, the direction it takes. By virtue of psychiatric medication and attention to psychology—

Pastor Reinhart paused a moment, then resumed.

"What I mean is, by giving attention to the biological we can take care of certain symptoms; but if the mind/soul/spirit continuum and the physical body really do influence each other you might treat the physical ailments but not attend to the spiritual component."

"Spiritual needs must be addressed," I said. "I feel that people with mental illness need the church. The power of corporate prayer and the fellowship of like-minded believers could help many to recover."

"Absolutely! I agree one hundred percent. When a person is battling for life, for wholeness, they need connection to the church, the body of Christ. Those who are suffering from an illness and are in a threatened condition can draw strength from the body—

Music suddenly erupted from the computer and we laughed. Pastor Reinhart got up from his chair to turn it off.

"I don't know why it's doing this," he said as he clicked the mouse.

"It has a mind of its own," I said and smiled.

"The mind in the machine, right?" Pastor Reinhart said.

We laughed again and then went on to discuss the articles on transpersonal psychology I had given him a week before my appointment.

"I really like some of the ideas in transpersonal psychology," I said. "For example, it advocates going beyond the narrow physiological stance that exists in modern psychiatry. In Western culture much of the psychiatric community has dictated that drugs are everything as though they will solve all our problems. But this literature indicates that there are altered states of consciousness that may need to be dealt with in other ways."

"Boy, I wonder what a psychiatrist would do with St. Paul!" Pastor Reinhart said. "In the book of Acts he talks about having had an experience of visions and revelations of the Lord. And he doesn't seem to say that it was caused by an extreme condition of his body. So here, within scriptures and within the church we've heard of visions and we haven't said, 'Well, Paul, he was crazy!' Paul had this mysterious experience of God. His religious experience pointed to a relationship with Christ. This can be true for us as well."

"The book of Acts is full of visions as well as other extraordinary experiences of a spiritual nature," I said.

"I think there are some interesting implications for us, that we may actually make ourselves more vulnerable by not accepting this spiritual reality," Pastor Reinhart said. "I think of my own experience—I've certainly had what I would call spiritual encounters. Most of mine have been in dreams and have been mostly positive over the years. But when I was thirteen years old I had what doctors call 'night terrors.' I don't deny the physiology of those but I would have real trouble convincing myself that it wasn't a real encounter with a spiritual power beyond me that was trying to kill me, kill me within a dream I was having one night. I was powerless before this presence that was suffocating me, then all of a sudden I recognized that another spirit entered into this struggle and ultimately overcame the first. I awakened deeply terrified and had to try to make sense of what happened."

"Oh, I believe it was a spiritual encounter but there are many who would say, 'You're just crazy, imagining things like that.'"

"I've had other dreams since then that have been at the minimum very vivid and possibly much more meaningful than that. And certainly, Christianity has voted through its history that these experiences are real."

"It has?" I asked.

"Oh, I think so. If you look through 2,000 years of Christianity, have we given credence to the existence of the life of the spirit and spiritual battle and these kinds of experiences? Yes, we have. It is a part of what it means to be human. As long as humans live their earthly lives they will have to face spiritual battles and that's why it is paramount to have God on one's side. Without God, well...."

Eventually our talk came to an end. I gathered my things and thanked Pastor Reinhart for his time. As I left his office I felt grateful for his intelligent, honest, and straightforward responses to my inquiries—responses which also reflected a compassionate and nonjudgmental attitude toward people with mental illness.

I was to find other Christians who viewed psychosis from the religious perspective. One was a friend who sent me a letter one day. In part, it read:

> Dear Marcia,
> I am most grateful for our infrequent visits....God, indeed, often uses voices,

visions—for you a rainstorm—to provide communication with His eternal desire that each of us surrender to His love, the love of a God who never forsakes us....

CHAPTER 22

Little by little and, step by step, I took on new responsibilities and commitments. After the time of setting up coffee for the weekly Bible study I signed up to give a presentation. I had two weeks in which to prepare and took the task very seriously. It was supposed to fill between twenty and thirty minutes and be based on Bible verses. My topic was forgiveness—something particularly appropriate for me to study.

The morning of my talk I joined the group for the usual sequence of events, i.e., announcements, singing, and prayers. Those gathered were mothers, grandmothers, career women, and housewives from all economic levels and both Protestant and Catholic backgrounds.

The coordinator called me forward. Standing behind a wooden podium with a cross on the front I looked out at the gathering of thirty or so women. They sat in tranquil silence, faces alert in expectation and polite receptiveness. Several opened their Bibles and one searched for a pen in her purse. I adjusted the microphone, took a deep breath and with my voice slightly wavering, began.

The scripture for today is—

"Could you speak a little louder please?" a white-haired woman requested from the back row. She apologized for the interruption.

I explained the meaning of a parable from the gospel of Matthew and said that: *According to the Bible, whether we forgive others or not is extremely important to God. In Ephesians 4:32 it says: "Be kind and compassionate to one another, forgiving one another, just as in Christ God forgave you."*

For the Christian, taking revenge is not an option, as in Romans 12:17 it says, "Do not repay anyone evil for evil." Since God forgives our transgressions, can't we have mercy on others? Sometimes we need to ask God to change our hearts, but for this to happen we must first realize how dependent we are upon God. The more we recognize our own faults and frailties, the more we realize how dependent upon God we truly are. And it is when we see the weaknesses within ourselves that we see our interconnectedness with all men and women everywhere....Mother Teresa of Calcutta used to claim that she engaged in her ministry of love because she knew there was a Hitler inside of her. In other words, the more we acknowledge our own sin, the more merciful and forgiving we will be toward others. The more we see our own imperfections, the more humble and less judgmental we will be....

*

So I decided to forgive Scott for all the years of abuse, for threatening me with a knife, pushing me down the stairs, etc. I forgave my parents for our lack of communication. I began to see the frailties and brokenness in my relative's lives from which they had suffered which, in turn, had had an impact on my own. I saw our desperate struggles as part of the human condition, something we all have in common. And I realized that I must forgive others as I have been forgiven. This included those I had encountered in the Unification Church and those who treat me with stigma and rejection. But I found I was only able to forgive from my heart when I asked God to fill my heart with forgiveness. This, he did.

And forgiveness brought healing. Not healing in the sense that all is forgotten—emotional and physical violence once branded into my heart will never disappear. But God enabled me to do what I once thought impossible.

There were other ways my faith had an impact on my daily life. Under oppression of sad moods, morning, noon, or night, I turned to prayer, reciting various passages from the Bible. I found Psalm 25 particularly comforting:

> To you, O LORD, I lift up my soul;
> in you I trust, O my God.
> Do not let me be put to shame,
> nor let my enemies triumph over me.
> No one whose hope is in you
> will ever be put to shame,
> but they will be put to shame
> who are treacherous without excuse....
>
> Turn to me and be gracious to me,
> for I am lonely and afflicted.
> The troubles of my heart have multiplied;
> free me from my anguish.
> Look upon my affliction and my distress
> and take away all my sins.
>
> Guard my life and rescue me;
> let me not be put to shame,
> for I take refuge in you....

My sadness would lift and I would be able to breath freely once again. I usually would have the same experience when listening to Christian music. Whether hymns or contemporary songs, they have brought me great joy and continue to be something I can rely on.

Call it being born again; call it new life in Christ; call it the joy of the Holy Spirit. Whatever its name, God is the provider, the divine source. But for me transformation has not been black and white—sick one day, healed the next. The path to restoration has been a process. Each morning, every night, I make the choice for health—to align myself, my thoughts and decisions, for the better life. And in my struggles that I will continue to face, I believe that I will have the true God as my defender, who is also my redeemer and friend. This is the victory, both temporal and eternal.

*

I was determined to let psychiatric professionals know how important it is to have an integrated approach to treatment for people with mental illness, an approach that encourages discussion of spiritual issues and problems. With this in mind I wrote a paper which was published in December of 2000.

Soon after, I was talking with an acquaintance, a psychologist and professor emeritus in the Department of Psychiatry at the University. He had read my article and said he was pleased that it was a study of phenomenology. He said that this approach to understanding and treating people with mental illness had been important before the 'biological revolution' in psychiatry.

[Phenomenology is the philosophical or scientific study of phenomena. In other words, the symptoms or manifestations of mental illness are described and studied with the hope of finding clues that would lead to the person's recovery.]

The professor said that in the early 1970's the psychiatry department went through a transition. Under a new department head research was shifted away from the study of phenomena to the biological root of mental illness and medications became the dominant mode of treatment. However, phenomenology is important and he was glad to see this perspective in my article.

It is important to treat the physical aspect of mental illness but not to the exclusion of other contributory methods. Often, psychiatric researchers must focus their proposals on material causes to receive funding, but in so doing, they generate reductionistic theories and, in this way, produce strong support for the biological model. While it is true that research has produced new medications that have improved the quality of life for many who have a mental illness, it is also true that psychosis, itself, has important meaning for those who've experienced it and that other interpretations of psychotic phenomena beyond the biological model matter.

CHAPTER 23

It was a fall day in 2000. Dr. Hayes and I were, again, seated in his office for a one o'clock appointment. To my right on the wall was a pastel painting of an ocean, rocky shore, and lighthouse. Books on various psychological and psychiatric topics lined a shelf to the left. Dr. Hayes did not have on his white coat today; he wore a stylish gray shirt with a navy tie. He began the session with a question.

"Do you think God can transmit His messages through psychosis?"

"Your use of the term 'psychosis' shows a mainstream traditional psychiatric view," I said. "I tend to have a more spiritual perspective. On the other hand, since you speak of God's communication, maybe you're not so mainstream after all."

Dr. Hayes looked thoughtful and was silent.

"There are people who believe that Jesus was psychotic but I believe that he really heard the devil speaking to him, for instance when he was tempted in the desert. I also know that hallucinations have to do with biochemical dysfunctions in the brain, but association is not necessarily causation. Dr. Hayes, does anyone really know the source of mental phenomena?"

"You shared one of Stanislav Grof's articles with me a while back. I think he uses an excellent analogy to describe his theory of consciousness."

"Yes," I said, "he says to consider the television set. You can't find the source of its programs by examining the physical parts that make up the TV. Peter Jennings is not inside the set, he's in New York. According to Grof, the TV 'simply mediates the program, it does not generate it.' C.S. Lewis, in *MIRACLES,* offers a similar analogy. We won't find the radio announcer in the radio itself. Along these same lines he says the mind's act of reasoning is a supernatural event and does not have its origin in the brain."

I explained to Dr. Hayes, applying Lewis' concepts, that even if the biological brain had an infinite number of neurons, these neurons could never give rise to the mental acts of comprehension, insight, or knowing. Lewis says that the chain reaction of "B followed A" [as one neuron's reaction to another] can never spawn the insight of "because of A, then B" which is an act of reasoning. Rational events such as acquiring insight or acts of knowing cannot have nonrational origins. In other words, the nonrational organic matter of the brain cannot be the source of the rational mind in the act of reasoning.

"There is thinking and then there is thinking *about* those thoughts," Dr. Hayes said. "Science has tried to reduce the mind to activity in the brain but I would agree that the mind is a different phenomenon; it is something other than chemical reactions even though it is related to them."

"I've been meaning to ask—do scientists know how a chemical could turn into a hallucination?" I said.

"No—they have no idea."

"Then the relationship of how hallucinations are formed, perceived, and experienced and any chemical imbalance is not really known," I said. "Personally, I doubt that it *can* be known. So that leaves us with the two perspectives on psychosis: one spiritual and the other physical."

To which Dr. Hayes quickly responded, "I don't think it is just one way or the other. This is something we may never have the answer to."

I told Dr. Hayes that the literature I enjoy the most deals with philosophical questions related to religion and that I am happiest when focused on God.

"How has your life been going?" Dr. Hayes asked.

"I mostly have good days but sometimes at night I still have problems."

"What do you mean?"

"Once I heard on TV that most suicides are committed at night by people who have a mental illness—I can understand why. Sometimes, even though I no longer hear clear words I feel threatened. Especially at night, feelings often come over me and thoughts oppress my mind as though 'voices' surround me, shouting, yet I hear no sound."

"What do they seem to be saying?" Dr. Hayes asked.

"It feels like, 'Kill yourself! No one loves you!' That sort of thing."

I told him that when morning comes the threat passes and that since 1994 my religious faith had stood between me and further suicide attempts or hospitalizations.

I spoke a while longer about my activities and my need to get out of my apartment to be with other people every day. We discussed my writing projects and future goals. He gave me a prescription, I thanked him, and left.

> Marcia is pleasant and seems to be doing well. She is not very spontaneous, nevertheless, her mood appears to be good and she shows no outward distress. I see no paranoid tendency in her thinking but rather at times a marked sensitivity. Thinking is logical and goal directed. She is not delusional. Her insight and judgment are good. She tells me she needs to, on a daily basis, be out of her apartment and interacting with people or she gets lonely. She is significantly bolstered by her faith and participation in a local congregation. Articles she has written express a strong sense of purpose and belonging through her belief in God and her church. She has a meaningful spiritual life that has contributed to the stability and improved quality of life that she has experienced in

recent years. This will be important to her continued improvement.

Evidence is beginning to emerge that suggests that people who experience a mental illness who have a religious faith fare better than those who do not. One such study can be found in the article, *The Prevalence of Religious Coping Among Persons With Persistent Mental Illness,* by researchers at the Fuller Theological Seminary and University of California in Los Angeles. Other studies show that prayer may decrease depression and anxiety as well as increase overall functioning.

Boisen wrote that 'inner victory' eventually brings with it social reintegration. My new found friends within the Christian community brought this to me. But it would not have been possible without that first connection when, years ago, I met Dr. Hayes. As an instrument of God's love his compassion and care initiated the healing process. In spite of many setbacks he persevered showing he was in for the long haul.

How many patients recognize the sacrifice physicians often make to heal others? It took me a while to realize this. Looking back, I feel that Dr. Hayes did his best for me and taught by example that suffering doesn't have to be meaningless, it can be endured for a greater good. He was Christ's hand outstretched to me, picking me up when I fell, letting me know that even though the world might consider me unimportant I mattered to God and could find a purpose for my life.

When he retired I said farewell. At our last meeting it was hard for me to say good-bye. I know that in the psychiatric profession relationships are supposed to follow strict rules of objectivity. Dr. Hayes had broken those rules because I felt he sincerely cared about what happened to me and he went beyond the call of duty, often sacrificing his own comfort and peace of mind. Some of his last words were to give me strength as I faced an uncertain future: "Don't ever give up!"

Recovery from a mental illness doesn't necessarily mean reaching a specific goal but that improvement occurs as a transitional process. A person can have setbacks but these problems will most likely be temporary and the person may bounce back.

God has given me the ability to reason and put my thoughts into words. Through writing my life has reached a new dimension. It has not only helped me to feel stronger and more mentally stable, it is a way of reaching out and communicating with vast audiences. I hope to encourage others who suffer from a mental illness and, hopefully, psychiatric professionals who read my work will gain some insight as well.

Through providential events God intervenes to alter the course of human lives. He uses them to point individuals toward fulfillment, giving purpose and direction. Frederic Flach, in *FAITH, HEALING, and MIRACLES,* gives an apt description:

> When providential events take place…[they] offer a chance to profoundly affect the course of our lives….*The litmus test for their divine origin is where the journey takes us.*[italics mine] Inevitably they will take us closer to God's will, to find new strength, the fulfillment of personal gifts and talents, greater harmony and generosity in our relationships with others, a deeper knowledge of loving, a deeper sense of God Himself….

*

I stood with a friend outside the sanctuary before a healing service.

"The spirit helps to overcome physical problems," she said.

As a retired physician she had helped many who had been ill over the years.

"That's true," I said. "But I think some people mistakenly believe that once they start to follow a religious path they will not have anymore problems."

"There will still be hardship but God gives us strength."

I nodded and said, "Let's go in."

We sat near the windows midway to the front. A single spotlight was shining on the cross which had a white cloth draped across the horizontal beam.

After forty or so people took seats in the pews the service began. We sang, read scripture, and prayed.

"All who wish the anointing of oil and laying on of hands please come forward," the minister said.

I walked down the center aisle. When my time came I knelt in front of the pastor and a woman who was from the prayer ministry. The pastor placed oil on my forehead.

The woman placed her hands on my shoulders and said softly, "Lord, protect her from all harm."

The pastor gave a blessing and then I got up and went back to the pew. After a final song my friend and the rest of the group filed out but I remained seated. From an east wing of the church came the wail of an unhappy child in the daycare nursery, a plaintive cry of humanity, *Relieve us from our distress, have mercy upon us....*

I glanced up at the cross then closed my eyes.

> *Lord God*
> *For all the people who have a mental illness, especially for those who cannot find the words or speak for themselves, I offer this prayer:*
> *Please help your children—we who are broken, sick, disillusioned, weary, and without hope. We have lived as outcasts, as those despised and neglected. We seek solace in your presence and peace in your promise. You, who ordained the spark of life that created us, come to our aid; claim victory in our battles and be our fortress. Fill us with hope and grant us new beginnings. That in this way we can know you, be healed, made whole, and proclaim as the ancient psalmist did: "For you have delivered me from death and my feet from*

stumbling, that I may walk before God in the light of life." [Psalm 56:13]

*In Jesus Christ's name,
Amen*

Endnote

To order more copies of this book and for more information about Marcia A. Murphy visit: www.hopeforrecovery.com. Ms. Murphy is also a speaker. Those interested in having her present to their group or organization may contact her directly at: murphyma@mchsi.com.

www.ingramcontent.com/pod-product-compliance
Lightning Source LLC
Chambersburg PA
CBHW050759160426
43192CB00010B/1571